Copyright © 2020 by Clifford Publishing, UK

All rights reserved. No part of this book may be reprinted or reproduced or utilised in any form or by any electronic, mechanical, or other means, now known or hereafter invented, including photocopying and recording, or in any information storage or retrieval system, without permission in writing from the publishers.

First Printing, 2020

British Library Cataloguing-in-Publication Data

A catalogue record for this book is available from the British Library

ISBN 978-1-913558-00-0

Clifford Publishing

1 Dock Road, London

United Kingdom, E16 1AH

www.cliffordpub.com

LANGUAGES AND THE CONSISTENCY

Jing Li
Jie Fang

2020

Preface

The work described in this book is part of the "ENGLISH BEANS" project, which is an online English learning program. Its target is to help the students in Chinese primary and secondary schools to improve the English learning efficiency by using the cutting-edge technologies such as Natural Language Processing, Corpus, and Knowledge Graph. "English Beans" has a multiple-level hierarchical architecture and complex structure, and it also involves a variety of third-party modules and tools. Consistency, among different modules and tools, is therefore a key problem for the purpose of the integrity of "ENGLISH BEANS" project. EXPRESS (ISO 10303-11) language was introduced into the project to describe the relative knowledge, information, and data in a semi-formal manner. Checking, analysis, simulation work then would apply on this semi-formal level to guarantee the consistency and complete of the overall system.

A correct EXPRESS model should not only be syntactically correct, but also semantically complete and consistent. In this context, the definition of consistency is that there should be no conflicting constraints in the model so that the model and all its sub-components can correctly co-exist in an instantiation.

Current approaches to EXPRESS model checking focus on syntactic and language semantic checking and on checking instance data against model constraints. The approach covered in this book is different in that it considers the issues of semantic consistency by analysis of the EXPRESS model definition.

Consistency is in part the focus of several paradigms such as UML, OWL and Constraint Programming (CP). Addressing consistency issues in those paradigms requires formal semantics and reasoning technologies that can fully cover such formal semantics. The work described here uses these formal approaches, and more particularly Constraint Programming, to provide a consistency checking environment for EXPRESS models.

This book describes the approach, highlighting both its advantages and its shortcomings. Currently CP is proving to be successful in handling many, but not all, classes of consistency checks. It is itself a rapidly advancing field and improved capability, which will extend the useful coverage as far as EXPRESS models are concerned, is appearing.

EXPRESS Model Consistency Checker (EMCC) was developed as a means to experiment with the idea of checking EXPRESS models for consistency by using CP. Various examples and test cases, both hypothetical and realistic, have been examined using EMCC. Conclusions drawn from the exercises prove the feasibility of checking EXPRESS models for consistency by using CP. They identify some significant directions in which these ideas should be improved and further developed as well.

This book was composed by Ms. Jing LI and Dr. Jie FANG. Ms. Jing LI had been teaching English in Shanghai High School for twelve years, and also edited the English text book for Chinese Secondary school in Oxford Publishing House. She is a linguistic, focusing on Corpus, English learning. Ms. Jing LI was awarded Master degree from Shanghai Jiaotong University in 2005. Dr. Jie FANG have been architect in multiple domains, such as Banking and Insurance for twenty years and his research interests includes AI, Information Modelling, Natural Language Processing and Knowledge Graph. He was awarded Doctoral Degree from University of Manchester in 2005.

Table of Contents

1. CONSISTENCY: THE INTRODUCTION 1

   1.1 CONSISTENCY ISSUES 1

      1.1.1 Inconsistency: semantic conflict 1

      1.1.2 Static and dynamic inconsistency 2

      1.1.3 Consistency issues in a variety of languages 3

   1.2 THE BENEFITS OF CHECKING CONSISTENCY 3

   1.3 THESIS CONTENT AND STRUCTURE 4

2. CHECKING CONSISTENCY: A GENERAL VIEW 5

   2.1 A LANGUAGE: ITS SYNTAX, SEMANTICS AND FORMALISM 5

      2.1.1 Syntax 5

      2.1.2 Semantics 6

      2.1.3 Formalism 8

   2.2 CONSISTENCY CHECKING IN A VARIETY OF SPEFICIATION LANGUAGES 8

      2.2.1 UML+OCL 8

2.2.2 The OWL language 11

   2.3 THE CONSTRAINT PROGRAMMING PARADIGM 15

      2.3.1 Constraints 16

      2.3.2 Constraint Satisfaction Problems 16

      2.3.3 Constraint solving 18

      2.3.4 CP and consistency issues 20

2.4 SUMMARY 21

3. INFORMATION MODELLING IN EXPRESS AND CONSISTENCY

ISSUES 22

   3.1 INFORMATION MODELS 22

      3.1.1 Objects 22

      3.1.2 Attributes 23

      3.1.3 Relationships between objects 23

      3.1.4 Constraints on objects and their relationships 24

      3.1.5 What an information model is not 25

   3.2 THE EXPRESS LANGUAGE 25

      3.2.1 SCHEMA 27

      3.2.2 Data types 27

      3.2.3 ENTITY 30

      3.2.4 Attributes 31

      3.2.5 Generalization/specification 31

      3.2.6 Constraints 32

   3.3 EXPRESS MODEL BASED SOFTWARE ENGINEERING 34

   3.4 CONSISTENCY ISSUES IN EXPRESS MODELS 34

      3.4.1 Characteristics of inconsistency in EXPRESS models 35

      3.4.2 Inconsistency patterns 36

      3.4.3 Static/Dynamic Inconsistencies 37

   3.5 SUMMARY 38

4. CHECKING EXPRESS MODELS FOR CONSISTENCY 39

4.1 REVIEWS OF THE EXPRESS LANGUAGE: SYNTAX,

SEMANTICS AND FORMALISM 39

4.2 IDENTIFYING AN APPROPRIATE APPROACH FOR EXPRESS

MODEL CONSISTENCY CHECKING 40

    4.2.1 Approach 1 40

    4.2.2 Approach 2: OWL 41

    4.2.3 Approach 3: UML+OCL 43

    4.2.4 Approach 4: CP 44

4.3 CHECKING EXPRESS MODEL CONSISTENCY BY USING CP 45

    4.3.1 EXPRESS model formalization 46

    4.3.2 Checking EMFS specification for consistency 48

    4.3.3 Exporting results 49

    4.3.4 An example of EXPRESS model consistency checking 49

4.4 THE FORMAL AND MODEL-BASED CONSISTENCY

CHECKING DESCRIPTION 52

    4.4.1 Model level consistency checking specification 52

    4.4.2 Mapping specification in EXPRESS-X 53

    4.4.3 Model activity specification in EXPRESS-C 56

4.5 SUMMARY 57

REFERENCES 58

1. Consistency: the introduction

Language is the communication of thoughts and feelings through a system of arbitrary signals, such as voice sounds, gestures, or written symbols. The ability to use language for communication is one of the characteristics that distinguish human beings from animals. These are natural languages, such as English, French and Chinese. As Computer Science has developed, many computer languages have arisen, such as modelling languages, programming languages, query languages and formal specification languages. Each of these languages is a system of symbols and rules used for communication with or between computers.

Natural languages are so called because they evolve naturally. A natural language is whatever the members of a human community agree to use for communication among them. It has probably diverged from some parent languages over a prolonged period. It is typically very complex, possessing a large vocabulary, allowing speakers and writers to express extremely subtle shades of meaning. It might well be rich in ambiguities. This is tolerable because listeners and readers are intelligent [Watt].

In contrast, programming languages or specification languages in the field of Computer Science are artefacts. They have been consciously designed by a single computer scientist or by a small group at some specific time. A programming language is used to instruct an uncomprehending machine; a specification language is used to describe a system unambiguously and to be the contract between the users of the system and the implementers. Those two sorts of languages therefore must be simpler and more direct than natural languages. The kind of subtlety and ambiguity in natural languages must be avoided in programming or specification languages.

1.1 Consistency issues

A correct phrase of specification should not only conform to the syntax rules but also meet some requirements at the semantic level, including sufficiency, consistency, unambiguousness, completeness and minimality. Consistency is the specific requirement for semantic correctness which is the focus of the research described in this book.

Consistency stands for the condition of standing or adhering together, or being fixed in union, as the parts of a body. For a phrase to be consistent, all its subcomponents should be true simultaneously. Consider the following sentence in natural English, which demonstrates an example of inconsistency.

```
Please choose a man from a group of girls.
```

This English sentence describes an impossible state or an unimplementable behaviour. This sentence has two clauses; one is

```
choose a man
```

and the other is

```
from a group of girls
```

There is a contradiction between the clauses, because a man can never be a member of a group made up of girls. Those clauses do not have a common solution; in other words, they cannot be satisfied simultaneously. This conflict between sub-clauses makes a specification inconsistent.

On the other hand, a consistent description is in agreement with itself, coherent and uniform. There should be no contradictions between its sub-clauses, and all of its sub-clauses should be able to exist or be true together.

1.1.1 Inconsistency: semantic conflict

Consistency issues occur at the semantic level, not at the syntactical level.

From the perspective of syntax and grammar, the sentence, which demonstrates inconsistency, is fully correct, although any literate and reasonable people can identify that such a sentence is nonsensical. The inconsistency lies in its semantics.

1.1.2 Static and dynamic inconsistency

In this book, inconsistencies are classified as either static or dynamic. This classification will be helpful when identifying consistency checking ability in a variety of languages in the following chapters.

A specification may describe not only a static system, but also the dynamic activities that take place in a system. Therefore, consistency issues may occur in both the static properties and the dynamic activities of a system.

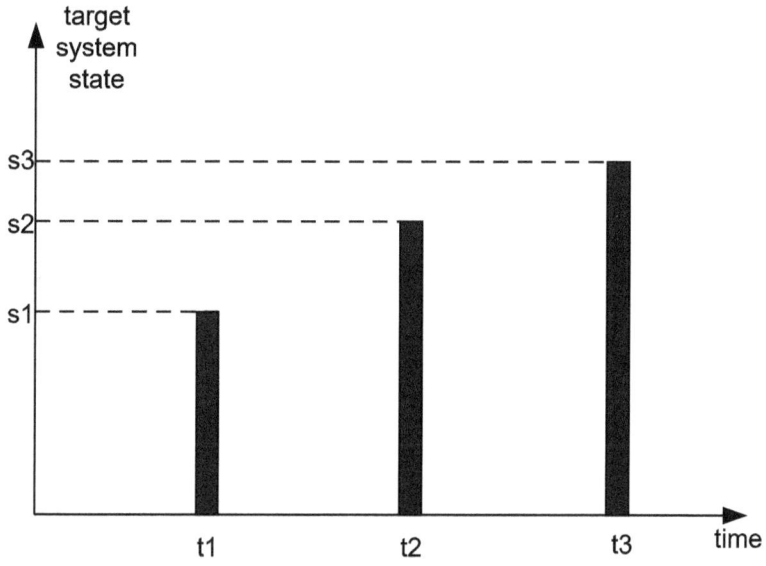

Figure 1.1 System Evolution

Figure 1.1 System Evolution illustrates that a system evolves as time goes by. The horizontal axis stands for time, and the vertical one stands for target system states. The target system is in state s1 at time t1, and will move to state s2, when time goes to t2, and finally will evolve to s3 when time goes to t3. s1, s2 and s3 are three snapshots of the target system taken at different times. The inconsistencies at the time of a single snapshot are static, and the inconsistencies among different snapshots are dynamic.

The following example shows a static inconsistency.

```
At 3:45 PM, John was in London. John was in Manchester at 15:45.
```

There is an inconsistency between the above two sentences. It is impossible for John to be in London and Manchester concurrently, because 3:45 PM and 15.45 denote the same time. These sentences describe a snapshot of John taken at 3:45 PM. The conflict between clauses was in London and was in Manchester is called *static inconsistency* in this book.

As noted above, there can be some dynamic inconsistency in a specification. The following example illustrates what, in this book, is called *dynamic inconsistency*

```
Mike was 15 years old last year, and he is 18 years old this year.
```

If Mike was 15 last year, he must be 16 this year. Alternatively, if he is 18 this year, he must have been 17 last year. The above sentence contains an inconsistency, because its sub-clauses cannot be true simultaneously.

These sentences are about something that evolves as time goes by.

Snapshot	Time	System state	System Evolution Rule
1	Last year	Mike was 15	A person grows one year older when one year passes by.
2	This year	Mike is 18	

Table 1.1 An Example of Dynamic Inconsistency

Table 1.1 illustrates two snapshots of the target system, one taken last year, and one this year. In snapshot 1, Mike was 15 years old, and Mike is 18 years old in snapshot 2. This target system is about people aging. There is an implicit system-evolution rule: A person grows one year older when one year passes by. In this case, a dynamic inconsistency exists between the two snapshots of the target system.

1.1.3 Consistency issues in a variety of languages

Consistency issues occur not only in natural languages, but also in the artificial languages in the field of Computer Science. Both programming languages and specification languages contain inconsistencies.

Many runtime errors in programs, such as infinite loops or array index overflows, can be regarded as inconsistencies. The following example is an excerpt of Java code:

```
for (int i=10; i<7; i++){
    ...
    ...
}
```

In the for loop structure, the loop variable i is initially set to 10, and will be incremented by 1 each time round the loop until i is less then 7. This piece of code can satisfy a Java compiler; but when running, the loop will never terminate, and will finally exhaust all resources and make the system collapse.

Snapshot	Time	System statues	System Evolution Rule
1	Initial	i=10	i:=i+1
2	Terminal	i<7	

Table1.2 Inconsistency in the Example Java Code

If the initial condition and the terminal condition of the `for` loop structure are regarded as two snapshots, the bug in this piece of Java code, which causes the infinite iteration, is then actually a dynamic inconsistency among the snapshots listed in Table1.2.

In the domain of Software Engineering, specifications or models are at least as important as programs when developing a big system. Some technologies including the Unified Modelling Language (UML) [OMG1999] [Fowler] [Schmuller] and formal specification languages, such as the B method [Abrial] [Lano], have been developed and used in system specification. Specifications in such languages can also contain inconsistencies. The following example shows an inconsistency in a specification written using the specification language in the B method.

```
MACHINE AgeSpecification
VARIABLES
    age
INVARIANT
    age = 1..100 ∧ age > 120
END
```

In the `AgeSpecification` machine, the invariants require the `age` variable to be both in a range of 1 to 100 and greater than 120. These two invariants conflict with each other and result in a static inconsistency. Chapter 2 will introduce more about consistencies in specification languages.

1.2 The benefits of checking consistency

Inconsistencies frequently occur in daily conversation and literature to emphasize emotion. For example, the phrase `Sun would rise from west` is always used in Chinese to express strong negation or denial. It is therefore not necessary to check consistency in informal speech and documents. However, inconsistencies must be identified and eliminated from official or formal documents such as legal documents. Consistency checking in natural languages is realized by proofreading.

In the field of Computer Science, program and specification verification is a research focus for the purpose of high quality software engineering. A verified program or specification is at a minimum consistent. When verifying programs or specifications, inconsistencies must be identified and eliminated.

As described in Section 1.1.3, many run-time-errors in programs can be regarded as inconsistencies. Consistency checking will therefore be helpful in developing high quality programs. Some groups and companies [ICL] [Chaltsev] exploit consistency theory in developing advanced compilers, which can to some extent identify runtime-errors in programs. These advanced compilers not only translate the program to executable code, but also verify and validate them before translation. Design flaws that otherwise might be discovered only during costly testing and debugging phases can be revealed at the programming and compilation phases. For example, the Formal Methods Group in the School of Computer Science, University of Manchester has been developing self-validating compilers [Voronkov]. The main objective of this research is to identify and remove inconsistencies at all levels in a program. With this approach, it is possible to develop high quality programs without runtime-errors in the future.

When developing a large software system, specifications will often be more important than programs. A variety of specification languages, formal or informal, have been developed and put to use. No matter what specification languages are used, inconsistencies should be identified and removed before implementation; otherwise, inconsistencies will move from the specification to implementation and become potential threats to the applied software. Consider the example in Section 1.1.3 again.

```
MACHINE AgeSpecification

VARIABLES
      age

INVARIANT
      age = 1..100 ∧ age>120

END
```

There is an inconsistency between the invariants in it. If some SQL code, such as

```
SELECT ... WHERE (age>0 AND age<100 AND age>120)
```

is generated from this specification, the generated SQL code will then contain errors and never work as it is designed to do. In this example, the SQL code will always return an empty result. Such errors will ruin the whole software project and even probably cause dangerous results if the software is used in a safety-critical environment.

1.3 Content and structure

The aim of this book is to investigate both consistencies in models[1] and specifications. In particular, the objective is the consistency issues in EXPRESS [ISO94b] models. In the field of computer science, there are various technologies, such as UML, the Web Ontology language (OWL) [W3Ca] and Constraint Programming (CP) [Marriott] [Fruhwirth], which to some extent can address consistency issues.

EXPRESS is an information modelling language. It focuses on describing the static structure of a target system at the definition level, although some instance level information is used to declare constraints. Therefore, most consistency issues in EXPRESS models are of the static type.

The research described in this book has not developed any new technology for EXPRESS model consistency checking, but instead has identified the most capable and suitable technology from the existing consistency related technologies and exploits it in the domain of EXPRESS models. Among UML, OWL and CP, CP was finally selected for EXPRESS model consistency checking, because of its consistency checking ability.

Chapter 2 describes consistency checking in a variety of specification and modelling languages. Chapter 3 introduces EXPRESS models and the consistency issues by which they can be affected.

---

[1] In this book, a model is *a schematic description of a system*. The other interpretations of this term such as the one in Formal Methods *a satisfying interpretation for a formula* are not applicable

2 Checking consistency: a general view

This chapter first examines the fundamental concepts of a specification language, covering issues of syntax, semantics and formalism. In Chapter 1, it was argued that consistency issues in a specification arise because of conflicts among clauses at the semantic level. It follows, therefore, that an activity such as consistency checking requires the language in which the specifications are written should itself have clear semantics. Moreover, the semantics must be formal, if the consistency checking activity is to be automated, but not rely predominantly on the efforts of people.

This chapter introduces consistency checking applied in a variety of specification and modelling paradigms, such as UML and OWL.

This chapter also introduces Constraint Programming (CP). CP does not address consistency issues directly, but if they are re-expressed, it allows them to be solved as constraint satisfaction problems (CSPs),

2.1 A language: its syntax, semantics and formalism

A language consists of signals, such as voice sounds, gestures, or written symbols, and rules for combining such signals to make a meaningful specification. A language may be considered at two levels: syntax and semantics. Syntax is concerned with the formation of phrases, whereas semantics concerns the meaning of phrases. Formalism of a language depends on whether it has a formal semantics.

2.1.1 Syntax

Each language has a vocabulary of symbols, and rules for how these symbols may be put together to form phrases.

The symbols of a natural language are words and punctuations marks. These are assembled to form phrases: noun-phrases, verb-phrases, clauses, and ultimately to form sentences. For example, `I see the green house.` is an English sentence, within which `the green house` is a noun-phrase. Not only the vocabulary but also the rules for forming phrases vary from one language to another. For example, contrast the English noun-phrase `the green house` (in which the adjective precedes the noun) with the corresponding French noun-phrase `la maison verte` (in which the adjective follows the noun). Furthermore, the utterance `the house green`, although composed entirely of English words, is not in fact an English phrase, since the words have not been assembled in accordance with the English rule for forming phrases. Thus syntactic rules define which phrases are well-formed and which are ill-formed [Watt].

In the field of Computer Science, languages can define their syntax either textually or graphically.

The symbols of a textual language in Computer Science are identifiers, literals, operator symbols, punctuation marks and so on. Again, these are assembled to form phrases: expressions, declarations, commands and ultimately to form a complete program or specification. The syntax of a language defines its valid symbols such as vocabulary and punctuation marks and the rules which should be conformed with when assembling the symbols to form phrases. The syntax of a textual language is defined in a formal notation such as the Extended Backus-Naur Form (EBNF) notation [ISO96]. It is then possible to develop syntax checkers for any specific textual language. For example, the Java language syntax in EBNF can be found in [Botting]. By using this syntax definition, it is possible to check whether a phrase is valid in Java. All Java compilers, such as Core Java J2SE 1.4 [Sun] and Jikes [IBM2004a], include checkers that automate the syntax checking activity.

In addition, there are some graphical specification or modelling languages. They use graphical icons instead of identifiers and literals as the basic symbols to make up phrases and specifications. UML, whose purpose is to present multiple views of a system, is a popular and commonly used graphical language. The UML syntax includes a number of graphical elements, and the rules for combining these elements to form diagrams. Figure 2.1 shows an example of the UML notation that captures the attributes and behaviour of a washing machine. A rectangle is the icon that represents the class. It is divided into three areas. The uppermost area contains the name, the middle area holds the attributes, and the lowest area the operations [Schmuller].

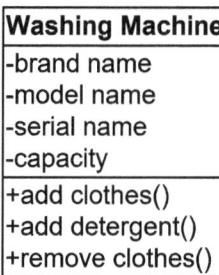

Figure 2.1 The UML Class Icon

Unlike the textual languages, there is not any formal notation which can be used for graphical language syntax definition. The syntax of a graphical language is recorded and explained in natural language. For example, Object Management Group (OMG) [OMG2004] issued OMG Unified Modeling Language Specification [OMG1999], which defines the syntax of UML in natural English. Because computers do not read in graphics, graphical specifications cannot be parsed and interpreted by computers directly. It is therefore impossible to develop any syntax checker like the ones for the textual languages. However, in Graphical User Interface (GUI) systems, it is possible to develop some templates which can help drawing syntactically valid graphical specifications. For example, Visio [Microsoft], Rational Rose Developer [IBM2004b] and Together [Borland] contain some templates or stencils for UML.

2.1.2 Semantics

Semantics specify the meaning of words, phrases and sentences in a language by stating how the symbols are put into a correspondence with the task domain. They permit the users to explain the meaning of sentences in the language in terms of the task domain. With this semantic commitment, users can discuss correctness, or truth, of phrases or sentences independently of how they are used [Poole].

The semantics of a word or a phrase is always represented as a mapping to the task domain or the other specifications. In a natural language, each word and each phrase has a meaning, namely the object, idea, or association that it conjures up. For example, the English word house denotes a particular kind of building;

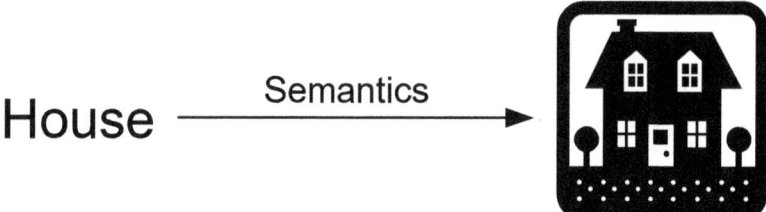

Figure 2.2 Semantics of the Word House

The semantics of the word House is expressed as a mapping to houses in the common sense, which is illustrated as an icon in Figure 2.2.

The semantics of programs or specifications can be represented as mapping to the task domains or the other specifications as well.

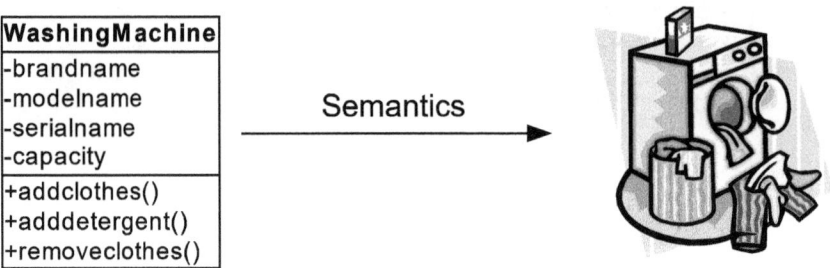

Figure 2.3 Semantics of the `WashingMachine` Class in UML

Everyone when reading the `WashingMachine` class in Figure 2.3, will think of washing machines in daily life. The semantics of such a class in UML is therefore represented as a mapping to washing machines in Figure 2.3.

Moreover, a word or a phrase can have multiple semantics. In other words, a specification can map to multiple objects in a variety of systems. In a natural language such as English many words in its vocabulary have multiple interpretations and map to multiple objects in the real world. For example, the English word `bank` has multiple interpretations, among which the most commonly used two are `business for keeping money` and `land along each side of a river`.

In the domain of Computer Science, a specification may be used for different purposes, such as documentation, code generation, verification and test. Therefore, the semantics of a specification will vary when mapping to different domains or interpreted by different users. For example, Figure 2.3 shows the semantics of the `WashingMachine` class is washing machines in daily life. However, when a mathematician is doing verification on this UML class, he will probably map that class to a set definition in Set theory and predicates in Logic. On this occasion, the semantics of the `WashingMachine` class is then set and predicate specifications in Mathematics. Therefore the `WashingMachine` class can have two sorts of semantics, and probably even more.

The following example illustrates that a program can have multiple semantics. Interpretation varies when different people read the code of a Java program.

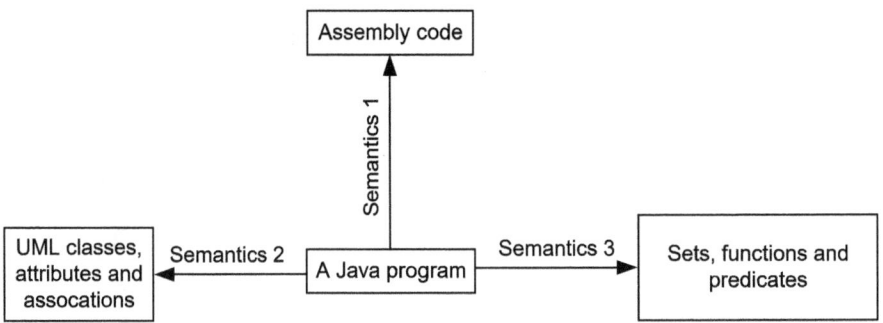

Figure 2.4 Multiple Semantics of a Java Program

There is a Java program in Figure 2.4. A compiler person interprets the idea of that Java program as some assembly code such as cache and register operations; a UML modeller interprets it as some classes, attributes and associations representable as a UML class diagram obtainable by reverse engineering; a mathematician or logician may interpret the concept of a Java program as some sets, functions and predicates in Logic. The code of a Java program therefore can be mapped to assembly code, to UML classes, attributes and associations, or to some specifications in Set theory and Logic, and probably to some other interpretations. The semantics of the code of a Java program are not unique and fixed.

In brief, the semantics of specifications or programs, which are represented as mappings to other domains, are not fixed, and may vary in different contexts.

2.1.3 Formalism

The use of the term *formal* as in formal definition, formal theory or formal semantics is often intimidating. Formal should really mean the opposite, namely that the definition is precise and the concept is well-defined without undefined terms. There should be no undefined terms. A proof should be possible just using the form of the definitions, without having to appeal to intuition about the subject matter [Poole].

For a language to be formal, it should have semantics on which some mathematical theory can be applied and reasoning is possible [Lamport]. Such semantics is called the formal semantics for that language. Section 2.1.2 stated that semantics of a language is represented as mapping to another domain. A language, for the purpose of being formal, should have some mapping defined, which relates it to some mathematical theories.

There are various formal specification languages. They are called formal specification languages because they have formal semantics. Those languages originated from Logic and Set theory, whose basic idea is to use Mathematics and Logic to describe target systems in order to guarantee their correctness [Wing]. These formal languages include Z [Spivey], the specification language in the B Method [Abrial], the specification language in Prototype Verification System (PVS) [SRI] and many others.

In addition to the formal specification languages, there are various informal ones, like UML. UML is the successor to the wave of object-oriented analysis and design methods that appeared in the late 1980s and early 1990s. It does not have formal semantics and this shortcoming limits deploying verification methods in UML specifications. Some groups are working on assigning formal semantics to UML. Consider for example U2B [Snook]; it formalizes UML specifications by mapping them to specifications in B.

Programming languages such as Java and C are not formal because they do not have semantics that are captured formally. Although some work has been done on assigning formal semantics to those programming languages (using an approach called formalization), no breakthrough has yet been achieved.

In general, formal semantics means precise and well-defined concepts and definitions, upon which a proof should be possible without having to appeal to external knowledge. The formalism of a language is dependent on whether it has a formal semantics. In order to gain verification and validation ability, some informal languages have been assigned formal semantics by an approach called formalization.

2.2 Consistency checking in a variety of specification languages

Consistency checking requires the identification of semantic conflicts. Moreover, if the checking activity is to be automated rather than rely on the efforts of people, the semantics of the language in which specifications are written should have formal semantics upon which some sort of proof or reasoning is possible. Inconsistencies occur in many languages, but only a few of them have made an effort to address inconsistencies.

This section introduces consistency and consistency checking in UML (Version 1.4) [OMG1999] and OWL. Each of the two languages is among the best-known representatives of a distinct and wide class of specification languages. On the other hand each is built with a distinct philosophy.

UML, an informal specification language, is distinguished by its full expressiveness in object oriented modelling and being easy to use and learn. However, the semantic ambiguity and overlapping in UML models may cause inconsistencies [André] [Gogolla]. Work [André] [Clark] [Evans] has been found on formalizing and validating UML models including consistency checking. It is therefore possible and necessary to study how consistency issues are handled in UML models.

OWL, which has Description Logic [Badder2003b] based formal semantics, is distinguished by being a third generation web language and supporting fully consistency and subsumption checking. It is therefore necessary to investigate consistency checking in OWL.

2.2.1 UML+OCL

UML is a widely accepted standard for object oriented modelling. The UML notation is largely based on diagrams. However, for a certain aspect of a design, diagrams do not provide the level of conciseness and expressiveness that a textual language can offer. Thus, textual annotations are frequently used to add details to a design. A special class of annotations are constraints that impose additional restrictions on a model. For this purpose, the Object Constraint Language (OCL) [OMG1999] provides a framework for specifying constraints on UML models. OCL is a textual constraint language with a notational style similar to commonly used object oriented languages [Richters2002]. Although OCL is a component of UML, the term UML+OCL is used in this book to emphasis UML models with OCL constraints.

A UML model provides the context for OCL constraints. Figure 2.5 shows a class diagram modelling employees, departments and projects.

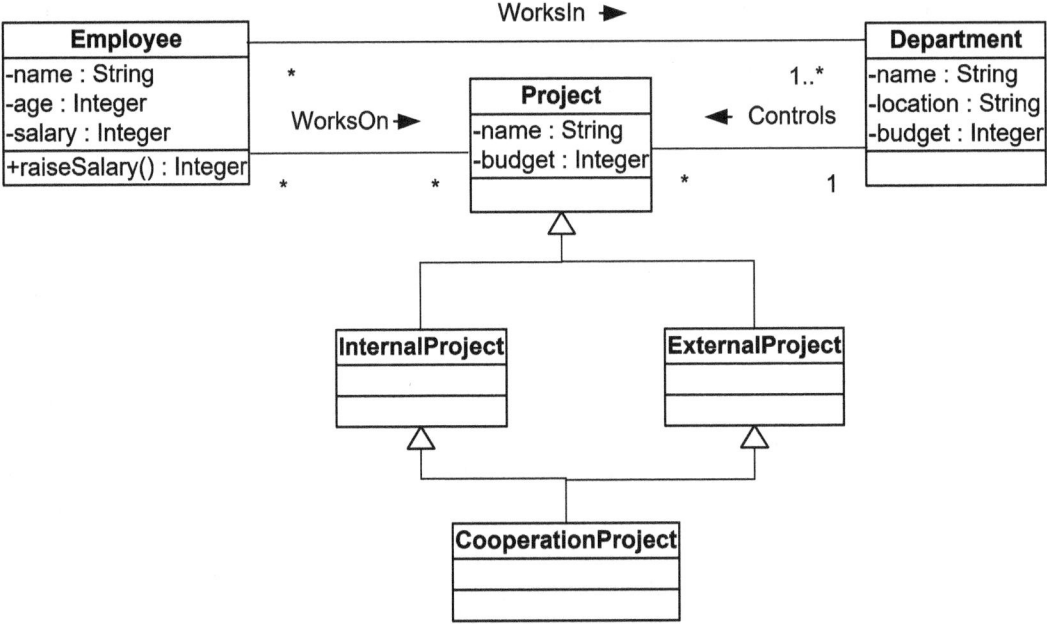

Figure 2.5 The UML Class Diagram of the Example Model

Attributes like name, age and salary represent properties that are common among all objects of a class. The operation raiseSalary can be invoked on employee objects. This is the only operation in the example model to keep it small. The operation signature defines a parameter and a return value of type Integer. Relationships between the classes are modelled as associations called WorksIn, WorksOn, and Controls. There are two kinds of projects: InternalProject and ExternalProject. CooperationProject is of both InternalProject and ExternalProject.

OCL can be used to specify constraints, specifically invariants, preconditions and postconditions, concerning both the static structure and the behaviour of a system [Richters2002] [Haime]. Invariants are static structure constraints. An invariant is a condition that must be true for all instances of that type at any time [OMG]. For example, the following invariant requires all department objects to have non-negative budgets.

context Department **inv**:

    self.budget >=0

More complex constraints can be built by navigating along the associations between classes, for example:

context Department **inv**:

    self.employee->forAll(e1,e2|

        e1.project->size > e2.project->size

        implies e1.salary > e2.salary)

The above invariant models that employees working on more projects than other employees in the same department get a higher salary.

The forALL expression asserts a condition for each pair of employee objects working in the same department. The expression e1.project yields the set of projects the employee e1 is working on.

The OCL standard operation SIZE determines the cardinality of that set. Role names like `project` and `employee` at the ends of the associations are omitted in Figure 2.5. If no role name is given, the default in UML is to use the class name starting with a lowercase letter.

The behavioural interface of objects is defined by operations. Constraints on the behaviour are specified in OCL by means of pre- and post-conditions. Such a constraint defines a contract that an implementation of the operation has to fulfil [Meyer].

```
context Employee:: raiseSalary(amount : Integer): Integer
    pre  : amount > 0
    post: self.salary = self.salary @pre + amount
        and result = self.salary.
```

The precondition in the above constraint specifies that the amount of the salary increase is positive, and the post-condition defines the result of the `raiseSalary` operation.

Although designed to be a formal language, a subset of Z [Warmer], experience with OCL has shown that the language definition is not precise enough. Various authors have pointed out language issues related to ambiguities and inconsistencies [Cook] [Gogalla] [Hamie].

Multiple invariants can be applied to a class in UML, and the constrained class will become inconsistent if the invariants conflict with each other. For example:

```
context Employee inv
    self.salary > 1000
    ....
context Employee inv
    self.salary <800
```

These two invariants constrain the employees to having a salary more than a thousand and less than eight hundred. They conflict with each other and make the `Employee` class inconsistent. This sort of inconsistency is of the static type which has been introduced in Chapter 1, because both of them constrain the same state of an `Employee` object.

Dynamic inconsistencies occur in OCL specifications as well. The precondition and post-condition of an operation represent the properties of a class at different times: before and after an operation. The inconsistencies between them are therefore dynamic. For example:

```
context Employee :: raiseSalary (amount : real) : real
    pre  : amount > 0
    post: self.salary = self.salary @pre + amount
        and self.salary < self.salary@pre.
```

The precondition requires the amount to be positive, but the postcondition requires that the salary after it has been raised should be less than before the rise was applied, Such an inconsistency, which is between the precondition and postcondition of the `Employee` class, is dynamic, because the precondition and postcondition are of different snapshots over time of an `Employee` object.

There are a variety of tools supporting the drawing of UML diagrams and features like code generation and reverse engineering. However, support for OCL and semantic analysis of models is rarely found in these tools. Table 2.1 shows a list enumerating the most important kinds of tools supporting OCL which is given in [Richters2002]. [Richters2002] distinguishes between tools doing:

1. Syntactical analysis
2. Type checking
3. Logical consistency checking
4. Dynamic invariant validation
5. Dynamic precondition/post condition validation

6. Test automation
7. Code verification and synbook.

Feature	Tool				
	Octopus [Klesse]	Dresden OCL Toolkit [Dresden]	Ein Interpreter for OCL [Wittmann]	ModelRun [BoldSoft]	USE [Richters2001]
1 Syntactical analysis	Yes	Yes	Yes	Yes	Yes
2 Type checking	No	Yes	Yes	Yes	Yes
3 Logical consistency checking	No	No	No	No	No
4 Dynamic invariant validation	No	No	Yes	Yes	Yes
5 Dynamic precondition/postconditon validation	No	No	No	No	Yes
6 Test automation	No	No	No	No	Yes
7 Code verification and synbook.	No	No	No	No	No

Table 2.1 Some OCL Tools and the Features They Support

Logical consistency checking in [Richters2002] is called static consistency in this book, and dynamic precondition/postcondition validation is equivalent to dynamic consistency in this book. Therefore, no tools have been identified that can check static consistency in OCL, and USE [Richters2000] [Richters2001] [Richters2002] is the only tool that can check dynamic consistency in OCL.

2.2.2 The OWL language

OWL, which stands for Web Ontology Language, is a World Wide Web Consortium (W3C) recommendation. Figure 2.6 illustrates some traits of OWL.

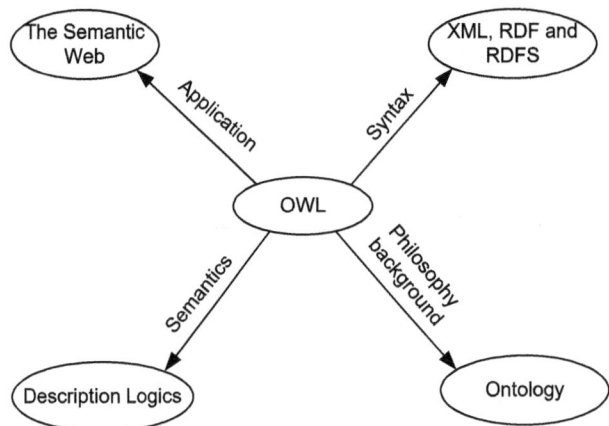

Figure 2.6 OWL

OWL is developed for the Semantic Web [SemanticWeb], which is the third generation Web. The World Wide Web (WWW) has been made possible through a set of widely established standards which guarantee interoperability at various levels. These include Transmission Control Protocol/Internet Protocol (TCP/IP) [Cisco], Hypertext Transfer Protocol (HTTP) [W3Cf] and HyperText Markup Language (HTML) [W3Cg]. The current Web can be characterised as the second generation Web: the first generation Web was characterised by handwritten HTML pages; the second generation made the step to machine generated and often active HTML pages. These generations of the Web are meant for direct human processing such as reading, browsing, form-filling. The third generation Web, the Semantic Web, aims to make Web resources more accessible to automated processes by adding meta-data annotations that describe their contents. If meta-data annotations are to make resources more accessible to automated agents, it is essential that their meaning can be understood unambiguously by such agents. Ontology [Sowa1999] will play a pivotal role here by providing a source of shared and precisely defined terms that can be used in such meta-data [Bechhofer].

In Information and Knowledge Science, ontology is the hierarchical structuring of knowledge about things by subcategorising them according to their essential (or at least relevant and/or cognitive) qualities. An OWL specification describes some terms in a domain, their attributes and relationships among them. These terms make up ontology and will work as meta-data accessible to automated process. Therefore ontology is the philosophical theory underpinning OWL.

OWL is a member of the Extensible Markup Language (XML) [W3Cb] family; in other words, it is an application of XML. OWL therefore complies with the XML syntax. OWL also makes use of the Resource Description Framework (RDF) [W3Cc] and Resource Description Framework Schema (RDFS) [W3Cd]. At the syntactic level, an OWL specification consists of some tags, including XML tags, RDF tags, RDFS tags and OWL tags.

High quality ontology is crucial for the Semantic Web, and its construction, integration, and evolution greatly depends on the availability of powerful reasoning tools with well-defined semantics. Since Description Logics provide both, they should be ideal candidates for representing the semantics of OWL. If Description Logics are chosen to serve as the formal semantics of OWL, checking an OWL specification for consistency can then be realized as reasoning and proof work in the domain of Description Logics.

The Information Management Group [IMG] in the Department of Computer Science, University of Manchester and some other research bodies have been working on, and contributing to, applying Description Logics to Ontology languages like OWL and the Semantic Web. Various algorithms and tools which implement such algorithms have been developed to check consistency and subsumption in OWL specifications, or more precisely in the formal semantics of OWL: Description Logics.

Description Logics are a family of knowledge representation languages that can be used to represent the knowledge of an application domain in a structured and formally well-understood way. The name Description Logics is motivated by the fact that, on one hand, the important notations of the domain are described by concept descriptions that are built from atomic concepts (unary predicates) and atomic roles (binary predicates) using the concept and role constructors provided by the particular Description Logic. On the other hand, Description Logics differ from their predecessors, such as Semantic Networks [Sowa2004] and Frames [Minsky], in that they are equipped with a formal, logic-based semantics [Badder2003a] [Badder2003b].

Description Logics are the decidable subsets of first-order logic. In order to ensure a reasonable and predictable behaviour of a Description Logic system, the inference problem should at a minimum be decidable for a Description Logic employed in the system, and preferably it should also be of low complexity. Consequently, the expressive power of Description Logics must be restricted in an appropriate way. If the imposed restrictions are too severe, however, then the important notations of the application domain can no longer be expressed. Investigating this trade-off between the expressiveness of Description Logics and the complexity of the inference problems has been the major issue in Description Logic research. [IMG] applied a typical Description Logic, $SHIQ$ [Horrocks], to OWL, and also developed a tool, **Fa**st **C**lassification of **T**erminologies (FaCT) [FaCT] which can do reasoning in $SHIQ$, to check consistency and subsumption in OWL specifications.

The following OWL specification describes the example in Figure 2.5, Section 2.2.1, which is about employees, departments and projects.

```
<owl:Class rdf: ID="Employee">
</owl:Class>

<owl:Class rdf: ID="Department">
</owl:Class>

<owl:Class rdf: ID="Project">
</owl:Class>

<owl:Class rdf: ID="InternalProject">
    <rdfs: subClassOf rdf:resource="#Project"/>
</owl:Class>

<owl:Class rdf: ID="ExternalProject">
    <rdfs: subClassOf rdf:resource="#Project"/>
</owl:Class>
```

```xml
<owl:Class rdf:about="#InternalProject">
    <owl:disjointWith>
        <owl:Class rdf:about="#ExternalProject">
    </owl:disjointWith>
</owl:Class>

<owl:Class rdf: ID="cooperationProject">
    <rdfs: subClassOf>
        <owl:Class rdf:about="#InternalProject">
    </rdfs: subClassOf>
    <rdfs: subClassOf>
        <owl:Class rdf:about="#ExternalProject">
    </rdfs: subClassOf>
</owl:Class>

<owl:ObjectProperty rdf:ID="WorksOn">
    <rdfs:domain>
        <owl:Class rdf:about="#Employee"/>
    <rdfs:domain/>
    <rdfs:range>
        <owl:Class rdf:about="#Project"/>
    <rdfs:range/>
</owl:ObjectProperty>

<owl:ObjectProperty rdf:ID="WorksIn">
    <rdfs:domain>
        <owl:Class rdf:about="#Employee"/>
    <rdfs:domain/>
    <rdfs:range>
        <owl:Class rdf:about="#Department"/>
    <rdfs:range/>
</owl:ObjectProperty>

<owl:ObjectProperty rdf:ID="Controls">
    <rdfs:domain>
        <owl:Class rdf:about="#Department"/>
    <rdfs:domain/>
    <rdfs:range>
        <owl:Class rdf:about="#Project"/>
    <rdfs:range/>
</owl:ObjectProperty>

<owl:DatatypeProperty rdf="name">
    <rdfs:domain>
        <owl:Class>
            <owl:unionOf rdf:parseType="owl:collection">
                <owl:Class rdf:about="#Employee"/>
                <owl:Class rdf:about="#Department"/>
                <owl:Class rdf:about="#Project"/>
            </owl:unionOf>
        </owl:Class>
    </rdfs:domain>
    <rdfs:range>
        <rdfs:resource="&xsd;string">
    </rdfs:range>
</owl:DatatypeProperty>

<owl:DatatypeProperty rdf="age">
    <rdfs:domain>
        <owl:Class rdf=about="#Employee"/>
```

```xml
        </rdfs:domain>
        <rdfs:range>
            <rdfs:resource="&xsd;integer">
        </rdfs:range>
</owl:DatatypeProperty>

<owl:DatatypeProperty rdf="salary">
        <rdfs:domain>
            <owl:Class rdf=about="#Employee"/>
        </rdfs:domain>
        <rdfs:range>
            <rdfs:resource="&xsd;integer">
        </rdfs:range>
</owl:DatatypeProperty>

<owl:DatatypeProperty rdf="location">
        <rdfs:domain>
            <owl:Class rdf=about="#Department"/>
        </rdfs:domain>
        <rdfs:range>
            <rdfs:resource="&xsd;string">
        </rdfs:range>
</owl:DatatypeProperty>

<owl:DatatypeProperty rdf="budget">
        <rdfs:domain>
            <owl:Class>
                <owl:unionOf rdf:parseType="owl:collection">
                        <owl:Class rdf:about="#Department"/>
                        <owl:Class rdf:about="#Project"/>
                </owl:unionOf>
            </owl:Class>
        </rdfs:domain>
        <rdfs:range>
            <rdfs:resource="&xsd;integer">
        </rdfs:range>
</owl:DatatypeProperty>

<owl:Restriction>
        <owl:onProperty rdf:resource="#WorksIn">
        <owl:minCardinality>
            1
        </owl:minCardinality>
</owl:Restriction>

<owl:ObjectProperty rdf:ID="Controls">
        <rdf:type>
            <owl:FunctionalProperty/>
        </rdf:type>
</owl:ObjectProperty>
```

Classes like Employee and InternalProject in UML diagram are represented as classes with the same id in OWL. Attributes like name and age are represented as DatatypeProperty in OWL. Associations like WorksIn are represented as ObjectProperty in OWL. Dynamic activities in UML such as the raiseSalary method are out of the scope of OWL and are ignored.

OWL cannot represent the OCL constraints which are attached to the UML diagram in Figure 2.5. However, OWL supports declaring some other sort of constraints, which constrain object existence and what classes objects belong to. For example, it is possible to declare the disjointWith relationship among classes.

The following excerpt in OWL declares the `disjointWith` relationship between the `InternalProject` and `ExternalProject` classes.

```
<owl:Class rdf:about="#InternalProject">
    <owl:disjointWith>
        <owl:Class rdf:about="#ExternalProject">
    </owl:disjointWith>
</owl:Class>
```

Thus the `InternalProject` class and the `ExternalProject` classes are mutually exclusive. There will not be an object whose type is of both these two classes. This constraint conflicts with the `CooperationProject` class which inherits both the `InternalProject` and `ExternalProject` classes. This specification in OWL does not pass the FaCT checker. The checker will identify that the `CooperationProject` will never be instantiable.

In brief, OWL with the support from Description Logics, can reason about the specification for consistency. However, this reasoning ability so far only covers classes and objects, not data types and values.

2.3 The Constraint Programming Paradigm

Constraint Programming (CP), and in particular, Constraint Logic Programming (CLP) has a multi-disciplinary nature; it embraces facets of Artificial Intelligence [Nilson], Logic Programming [Bratko], Operational Research [Taha], Numerical Computation [Pozrikidis] and Mathematical Programming [Wiliams]. It is one of the most exciting developments in computing languages of the last decade. Based on a strong theoretical foundation, it is attracting widespread commercial interest. Not surprisingly therefore CP has recently been identified by the Association for Computation Machinery (ACM) [ACM] as one of the strategic directions in computing research [Marriott] [Fruhwirth].

Within the context of Artificial Intelligence and Operations Research, Constraint Satisfaction Problems (CSPs) and Constraint Solving were investigated as long ago as the 1970s, before Constraint Programming was developed. The first modern constraint programming languages, Constraint Logic Programming (CLP) languages [Jaffar] were extensions of logic programming. These include CLP(R) [Jaffar], CHIP [Dincbas] and Prolog III [Colmerauer]. CLP was a natural combination of two declarative paradigms: constraint solving and logic programming. This makes constraint logic programs more expressive, flexible and in general more efficient than logic programs [Fruhwirth]. Inspired by the success of CLP, several other classes of CP languages have recently been suggested. These include: concurrent constraint languages which use constraint entailment to extend CLP by providing asynchronous communication between agents; constraint query languages for databases which extend relational databases by allowing tuples that contain constraint variables. Other examples include constraint functional programming languages, constraint imperative programming languages, and object oriented constraint solving toolkits. CLP languages are, however, the archetypal CP languages [Marriott].

The use of constraint programming supports the complete software development process. Because of its conceptual simplicity and efficient executable specifications, rapid prototyping and ease of maintenance are achieved. Since the beginning of the 1990s, constraint-based programming has been commercially successful. In 1996, the worldwide revenue generated by constraint technology was estimated to be of the order of 100 million US dollars [Fruhwirth]. The technology has proven its worth in a variety of application areas, including decision support systems for scheduling, timetabling, and resource allocation [Fruhwirth]. For example, the system Daysy [Lufthansa] performs personnel planning for Lufthansa after disturbances in air traffic, such that changes in the schedule and costs are minimized. Nokia uses CP for the automatic configuration of software for cell phones [Fruhwirth]. The car manufacturer Renault has been employing CP technology for production planning since 1995 [Fruhwirth].

CP is built upon CSPs. Therefore, some knowledge of CSPs is needed to fully understand the CP paradigm. This section describes the methodologies used for constraint solving. It concludes by establishing the relationships between CP and the kinds of consistency issues of relevance in the work described here.

2.3.1 Constraints

The idea of constraint-based programming is to solve problems by simply stating constraints (conditions, properties) which must be satisfied by a solution of the problem. For example, consider a bicycle padlock number. Suppose the owner forgets the first digit of the number, but remembers some constraints about it: The digit was an odd number, greater than 1, and not a prime number. By combining the pieces of partial information expressed by these constraints: digit, greater than one, odd, not prime, it is possible to derive that the digit the owner is looking for is "9". Constraints can be considered as pieces of partial information. Constraints describe properties of objects and relationships between them.

In the CP paradigm, constraints are formalized as distinct predefined predicates in First Order Logic (FOL). Constraints allow for a finite representation and efficient processing of possibly infinite relations. For example, each of the two arithmetic constraints X+Y=7 and X-Y=3 admits infinitely many solutions over the range of integers. Taken together, these two constraints can be simplified into the solution X=5 and Y=2 [Fruhwirth].

2.3.2 Constraint Satisfaction Problems

Constraint Satisfaction Problems (CSPs) appear in many areas, including, for example, vision and resource allocation in scheduling and temporal reasoning [Tsang].

Basically, a CSP is a problem composed of a finite set of variables, each of which is associated with a domain, and a set of constraints that restrict the values the variables can simultaneously take. The task is to assign a value to each variable such that all the constraints are satisfied [Tsang].

The formal definition of CSP is a triple: (**Z, D, C**)

Z: a finite set of variables $\{x_1, x_2, ... x_n\}$;

D: a function which maps every variable in **Z** to a set of arbitrary type:

$$D: Z \rightarrow \text{set of objects (of any type)}$$

D_j is the set of objects mapped from x_j by D. These objects are possible values of x_j, and D_j is the domain of x_j.

C: a set (possibly empty) of constraints on an arbitrary subset of variables in **Z**.

A solution of a CSP is a string of values: $<v_1, v_2, ..., v_n>$ which satisfies the following two requirements:

$$\{v_1 \in D_1, v_2 \in D_2, ..., v_n \in D_n\}$$

$$\{x_1 = v_1, x_2 = v_2, ... x_n = v_n\} \Rightarrow \forall c \in C \bullet Satisfies(c)$$

Each value in the string must be in the corresponding set, and if the variables are substituted by the corresponding values, all constraints must become satisfiable.

A CSP is satisfiable if a solution exists.

To formalize a problem as a CSP, it is necessary to identify a set of variables, a set of domains and a set of constraints.

The N-queens problem is a well known puzzle among computer scientists. Given any integer N, the problem is to place N queens on N distinct squares on an $N \times N$ chess board, satisfying the constraint that no two queens should threaten each other. The rule is that a queen can threaten any other pieces on the same row, column or diagonal. Figure 2.7 shows one possible solution to the 8-queens problem.

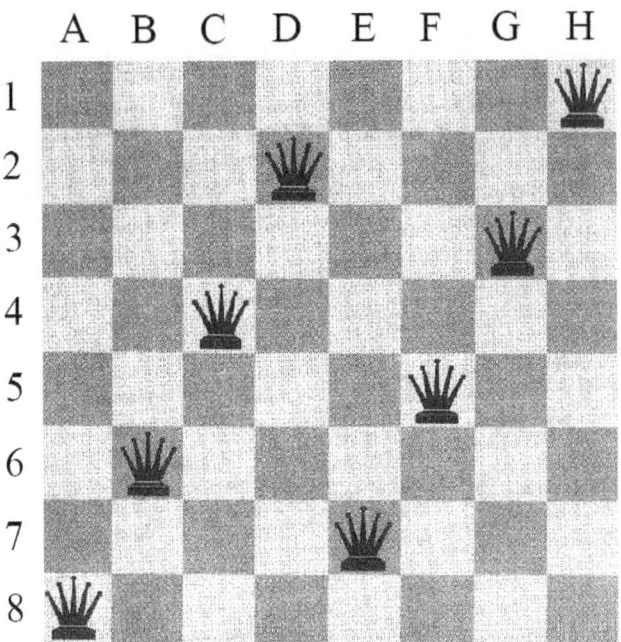

Figure 2.7 One Solution to 8 Queens Problem

One way to formalize the 8-queens problem as a CSP is to make each of the eight rows in the 8-queens problem a variable: the set of variables $\{x_1, x_2, ..., x_8\}$. Each of these eight variables can take one of the eight columns as its value. If the columns are labelled with values 1 to 8, then the domain of all the variables in this CSP are as follows:

$D_1 = D_2 = ... = D_8 = \{1,2,3,4,5,6,7,8\}$.

Now consider the constraints. The fact that each row is represented as a variable has ensured that no two queens can be on the same row. To make sure that no two queens are on the same column, the following constraint is used:

Constraint (1). $\forall i, j \bullet x_i \neq x_j$, which states that for subscripts i and j, x_i and x_j are not equal.

To make sure that no two queens are on the same diagonal, the following constraint is included:

Constraint (2). $\forall i, j \bullet (i - j \neq x_i - x_j) \land (j - i \neq x_i - x_j)$, which states that for subscripts i and j, the difference between i and j is not equal to the difference between x_i and x_j.

Therefore the 8-queens puzzle is formalized as the following CSP:

$Z : \{x_1, x_2, ..., x_8\}$

$D_1 = D_2 = ... = D_8 = \{1,2,3,4,5,6,7,8\}$

$C : \{(\forall i, j \bullet x_i \neq x_j), (\forall i, j \bullet (i - j \neq x_i - x_j) \land (j - i \neq x_i - x_j))\}$

There are several sorts of CSPs, according to the domains that the variables are in. If the constrained variables are in the Boolean domain, then that CSP is a Boolean one. The following example is a Boolean CSP.

$Z : \{p, q\}$

$D : Boolean$

$C : \{p \land q, p \lor q\}$

The variables in the above CSP are p and q. The variables are associated with the Boolean domain. The constraints that restrict the variables are: $p \land q$ and $p \lor q$.

If the constrained variables are integers, then the CSP is an integer one. The following example is an integer CSP.

$Z : \{w, v\}$

$D : INTEGER$

$C : \{w > v, w + v < 10, v \neq 8\}$

The variables in the above CSP are w and v. The variables are associated with the integer domain. The constraints that restrict the variables are: $w > v$, $w + v < 10$ and $v \neq 8$.

If the constrained variables are real numbers, then the CSP is of type real. The following example is a real CSP.

$Z : \{r, s, t\}$

$D : REAL$

$C : \{2 \times r + s \leq 16, r + 2 \times r + s \leq 11, r + 3 \times s \leq 15, t = 30 \times r + 50 \times s\}$

The variables in the above CSP are r, s and t. The variables are associated with the real domain. The constraints that restrict the variables are: $2 \times r + s \geq 16$, $r + 2 \times r + s \leq 11$, $r + 3 \times s \leq 15$ and $t = 30 \times r + 50 \times s$.

In addition to the above three sorts of CSPs, users can define their own domains in which the constrained variables exist. The user defined domains must be finite and subsets of the set of integers. Such CSPs are called finite domain CSPs. The CSP that formalized the 8-queens problem is an example of a finite domain CSP, because all variables are in $\{1,2,3,4,5,6,7,8\}$, a subset of integers.

2.3.3 Constraint solving

Constraint solving is to find satisfiability of CSPs. Obviously, the easiest way to apply constraint solving is to generate a possible solution, i.e., enumerate all possible values for the variables, and then to test if the constraints are satisfied. This is the so-called generate-and-test methodology used in Logic Programming. Unfortunately, this methodology is impractical in most cases. The problem is that this method only uses the constraints in a passive manner to test the result of applying values, rather than using them to infer values that form a solution.

A new methodology, the constraint-and-generate methodology [Fruhwirth], is applied in solving CSPs. In the constraint-and-generate methodology, first the constraints are applied to reduce the number of possible solutions and then a solution is generated. For example the solution of the following problem

$X \in \{1,2\} \wedge Y \in \{1,2\} \wedge Z \in \{1,2\} \wedge X = Y \wedge X \neq Z \wedge Y > Z$

is found after seven choices using the generate-and-test method, contrasting with the constraint-and-generate methodology where the solution can be found without making any choice, i.e., the constraint $Y > Z$ determines the values of Y and Z to be 2 and 1, respectively. Now, the constraint $X = Y$ propagates the information that $X = 2$ and the constraint $X \neq Z$ remains satisfied.

Many algorithms and strategies are applicable to constraint solving, but none of them is universal. Different solving algorithms and strategies will be applied to CSPs of different type and size. There are two main methods for constraint solving algorithms, problem reduction and solution synbook [Tsang].

2.3.3.1 Problem reduction

Problem reduction [Tsang] is a class of methods for transforming a CSP into problems which are hopefully easier to solve or recognize as insoluble. Although problem reduction alone does not normally produce solutions, it can be extremely useful when used together with searching or solution synbook.

With problem reduction, it is possible to remove the redundant values of the variables in the sets of a CSP. In other words, it can tighten the constraints. For example, consider the following CSP:

$Z : \{x, y\}$
$D_x : \{2,3,4\}, D_y : \{1,2,3\}$
$C : \{x < y, x + y = 4, x - y = 1\}$

The first constraint $x < y$ requires x to be less than y, then all values in D_x that are greater than or equal to the greatest value in D_y can be removed. Similarly, all values in D_y that are smaller than the smallest value in D_x can be removed. Therefore, after applying the problem reduction method on this CSP, its equivalent is generated:

$Z : \{x, y\}$
$D_x : \{2\}, D_y : \{3\}$
$C : \{x + y = 4, x - y = 1\}$

The generated equivalent is then an easier problem to solve. It can easily be identified that it is unsatisfiable, for x and y, if substituted by the corresponding values 2 and 3 cannot satisfy the constraints.

Problem reduction can also eliminate variables from CSPs to make them easier to solve. One well-known variable elimination algorithm is Gaussian elimination [MathWorld] for solving linear polynomial equations. Consider the example of the following CSP:

$Z : \{x, y\}$
$D : INTEGER$
$C : \{x = 7 - y, x = 3 + y\}$

By using Gaussian elimination, the second occurrence of x can be removed. This will result in $C : \{x = 7 - y, y = 2\}$. Removing y finally leads to the solution $\{x = 5, y = 2\}$ [Tsang] [Fruhwirth].

Generally, problem reduction methods transform CSPs to equivalent, but hopefully easier problems by reducing the number of variables and constraints or the size of domains.

2.3.3.2 Solution Synbook

Solution synbook is a class of methods used to generate all possible solutions to a CSP. That is, all assignments of values to variables that satisfy the constraints are produced by a solution synbook algorithm.

When searching for a solution to the following CSP:

$Z : \{x_1, x_2, ... x_n\}$
$D : D_1, D_2, ..., D_n$
$C : \{C_1, C_2, ..., C_m\}$

The method starts by assigning a value v_i to a variable x_i in Z, which satisfies all the constraints. Value v_i and variable x_i consist of a tuple $< x_i, v_i >$ called a partial solution to the current CSP. This partial solution is then extended by adding one tuple to it at a time, until all variables in Z are assigned valid values that satisfy all constraints in C. At that point, the partial solution becomes a real solution to the CSP. Solution synbook collects the sets of all legal values for larger and larger sets of variables, until this is done for the sets of all variables [Tsang][Beale][Freuder][Tsang1990].

Consider the following CSP:

$Z : \{x, y, z\}$
$D : INTEGER$
$C : \{x > 1, y > x + 12, z < y - 14\}$

Solving this CSP by using the solution synbook method involves three steps.

```
STEP(1) : partial_solution(1): {x=2};
```

In STEP(1), value 2 is assigned to variable x, all constraints that refer to x are satisfied. The partial solution is {x=2}.

```
STEP(2) : partial_solution(2): {x=2, y=15};
```

In STEP(2), value 15 is assigned to variable y, all constraints that refer to x and y are satisfied. The partial solution increments to {x=2, y=15}.

```
STEP(3) : partial_solution(3): {x=2, y=15, z=0};
```

In STEP(3), value 1 is assigned to variable z, all constraints that refer to x, y and z are satisfied. The partial solution increments to {x=2, y=15, z=0}.

Because all variables in Z have been assigned values such that all constraints in C are satisfied, the partial solution in STEP(3) is a real solution to that CSP.

The above example is naïve and only for demonstration purposes. A lot more detail on solution synbook can be found in [Tsang] and [Freuder].

2.3.4 CP and consistency issues

Although CP is not a specification language, and does have consistency issues that the specification languages such as UML have, it can be used to re-express and address consistency issues.

Figure 2.8 illustrates that a consistency issue can be interpreted as a CSP. Consistency issues are the conflicts among clauses in a specification at the semantic level. If the clauses in a specification are regarded as constraints in a CSP, the consistency among those clauses and the satisfiability of that CSP are equivalent.

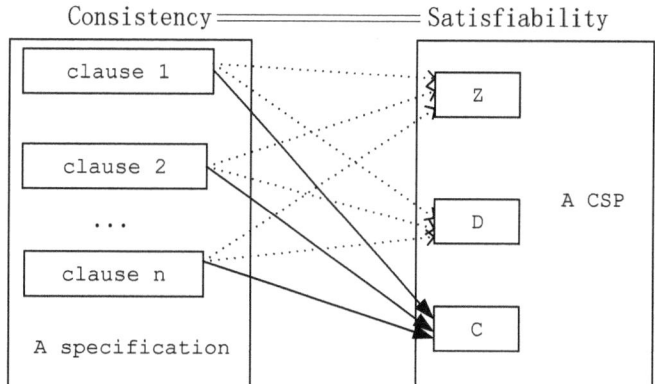

Figure 2.8 Re-expressing Consistency of a Specification as Satisfiability of a CSP

For example of the specification in B from Section 1.1.3.

```
MACHINE AgeSpecification
VARIABLES
      age
INVARIANT
      age = 1..100 ∧ age > 120
END
```

The inconsistency between the invariants in that specification can be re-expressed as the following CSP:

$Z : \{age\}$

$D : INTEGER$

$C : \{1 \leq age \leq 100, age > 120\}$

The unsatisfiability of this CSP reflects the inconsistency in the original specification in B.

The equivalence between consistency and satisfiability shows a hint of consistency checking. Consistency issues in a specification can be addressed via checking the satisfiability of the CSPs extracted from that specification.

2.4 Summary

This chapter has introduced language from the perspectives of syntax and semantics, and explained formalism of languages. It has also analysed consistency issues in UML and OWL, and shown how these issues can be handled. Consistency issues in formal languages to some extent are solvable. The consistency issues in informal languages can be addressed by the approach of formalization.

The technology of Constraint Programming has also been introduced. It can address consistency issues via solving Constraint Satisfaction Problems.

The consistency related technologies introduced in this chapter will be exploited in checking consistency in a particular modelling language, EXPRESS. The EXPRESS Language and the consistencies in EXPRESS models will be introduced in Chapter 3.

3. Consistency Issues in EXPRESS language

The preceding chapters generally described consistency issues in a variety of languages and the approaches to addressing them. This chapter moves the focus onto the consistency issues in a specific language: EXPRESS.

This chapter firstly introduces information models, and EXPRESS: an information modelling language used in the context of the work described in this thesis.

This chapter then systematically studies the consistency issues in EXPRESS models. Some characteristics and patterns of inconsistency in EXPRESS are presented.

3.1 Information models

An information model is a formal description of an area of interest (a domain). It specifies the objects within the domain, the relationships between the objects, the basic attributes of the objects, the constraints upon the objects and their relationships [Mint]. Its purpose is to identify clearly the objects in a particular "Universe of Discourse", and allow people to communicate more accurately about a domain of common interest.

An information model describes the static structure of objects and how they are related. It does not cover their dynamic behaviour. For example, it shows neither the interaction among objects, nor their transformation over time.

An information model should be a conceptual description which does not contain implementation specific details. This allows the information modeller to concentrate on the structure and semantics of the information, without also having to think about how it is going to be implemented.

An information model is more formal than a specification in natural language, it is understandable not only to people but also to computers. An information model therefore must be expressed in a language whose syntax can be formally defined, for example in the manner of ENBF. Hence, software tools can parse it for some further purpose such as automated code generation and software simulation.

In the following sections, the most important and widely accepted features that are required to describe information models are introduced. In the description, it is sometimes helpful to think about how an information model might be instantiated.

3.1.1 Objects

An important information modelling requirement is the ability to represent the objects of interest in the domain being modelled.

An object, in the context of software engineering, can only be created dynamically if there is a previously defined class. Hence, an object is an instance of a specified class; the types of its characteristics or attributes are declared in its class before its instantiation. For example, in an object-oriented programming language such as C++ or Java, before creating an object, the class to which it belongs should be defined.

This trait holds too for information models. An information model statically describes a domain of interest. It does not focus on a single object or instance but on an abstraction of a category of objects with some common characteristics. In other words, an information model does not define or create single objects, but focuses on the definition and abstraction of all possible objects in the domain and their categorization. A category of objects is often called an entity in information modelling languages.

Club Member				
Name	ID No.	Gender	**Address**	**Membership Type**
John Smith	0011239	Male	60 Pine Road	Gold
Yuki Lee	0011240	Female	3B Bigstone Building	Silver
Andrew Clark	0011241	Male	Flat 5 Fleet Garden	Silver

Table 3.1 Example of Club Member Information

There are three members of a club listed in Table 3.1. In the context of software engineering, they can be recognized as three objects, each of which has some characteristics such as a name, an ID number, a gender specification, an address and a membership type. However, an information model of this table does not focus on the different attribute values of these three members, such as `John Smith`'s ID No and `Yuki Lee`'s address, but on the abstraction of the information of all members. An entity, `club_member`, will be created to represent all members, and all specified members will be instances of it. Other entities, `club_member_gold` and `club_member_silver`, will be created too. They can represent the member status differences.

An entity should encapsulate all the information that is relevant to its target concept in the real world. It should also have an identifying name, which allows people who read the model to make a mental association between the model and its target in the real world.

3.1.2 Attributes

In an information model, an entity may have one or more attributes. The attributes describe the characteristics of the concept represented by the entity. Attributes are optional; an entity is valid without any attributes. An attribute should have a name that identifies the attributes and provides meaning to the reader.

The `club_member` entity that captures the information about the club members in Table 3.1 should have four attributes: `name`, `ID_number`, `gender` and `address`. The `membership_type` could also be captured as a generalization/specialization relationship between the `club_member` entity and the `club_member_gold` and the `club_member_silver` entities, see section 3.1.3.

Entities should only include the attributes that are relevant to the intended focus of the model. There are potentially an unlimited number of attributes that could be assigned to some entities. However, adding more attributes than is necessary will result in a large model whose important concepts are less clear. For example, the `club_member` entity may have some extra attributes such as `hair_colour` and `favourite_pop_group`, which are not necessary when considering the membership of a club, unless it is a pop music club. Including non-relevant attributes may affect the semantic clarity of the model and could lead to unnecessary work in any future implementation that conforms to the model.

3.1.3 Relationships between objects

There are two sorts of relationships between the entities of an information model: generalization/specialization relationships and association relationships.

The `club_member` entity is general, whereas the `club_member_gold` and the `club_member_silver` entities are more specific in terms of membership status. The generalization/specialization is created and maintained by the inheritance mechanism of the information modelling method.

Associations represent relationships between instances of entities. Each association has two association ends; each end is attached to one of the classes in the association. Associations typically include cardinality. It should also be possible to specify whether an ordering is required on the relationship.

Club Profile	
Club Name	Good Citizens Association
Club Address	113 Mary Street
Club Telephone Number	0161 222 8965
Club members	See the table of club member information

Table 3.2 Example of Club Profile

A `club_profile` entity can be made to capture the information shown in Table 3.2, which has four attributes: `club_name`, `club_address`, `club_telephone_number` and `club_members`. The `club_profile` entity has a relationship to the `club_member` entity; such a relationship can be represented as an association between those entities. One of the `club_profile` entity's attributes, `club_members`, will refer to the `club_member` entity. The `club_members` attribute plays the role of an association between the `club_profile` entity and the `club_member` entity. This association will be specified with a one-to-many cardinality, because a club can contain many members and must have at least one member.

3.1.4 Constraints on objects and their relationships

It should be possible to add constraints to an information model in order to describe the target system precisely and completely. A constraint is a rule that specifies further restrictions on the model. An instance of the information model must conform to all constraints in order to be valid. There are a number of different cases where constraints would be useful. This includes constraints that affect the attributes of an object, and constraints on the relationships between objects.

A reasonable constraint on the `club_profile` entity may be that the number of members must be more than one.

3.1.5 What an information model is not

An information model is a general concept compared with some others such as data model, program, documentation and interface.

An information model is not a data model, even though terms such as schema are used for both information models and data models. A data model focuses on the implementation, not on the conceptual design. It often reflects an implementation strategy, and is used in database management system design. Compared with a data model, an information model focuses on describing the semantics of the information and the relationships between information items. It does not focus on the implementation of the design. It is possible to use an information model as a data model in a data base related project. But information models can be used for many other purposes, as well as being data models.

An information model is not a program either. A program is a sequence of instructions that a computer can interpret and execute, whereas an information model is a piece of static description interpretable to both humans and computers. Although information modelling shares some programming concepts such as object orientation, it need not provide methods and is not compatible with executable computer programs [Horst].

An information model may be described textually or diagrammatically. The textual approach includes the Z method [ZN] and the EXPRESS language. The diagrammatic approach includes the Integration Definition for Information Modeling (IDEF1X) [IDEF98], EXPRESS-G and Unified Modeling language (UML).

The EXPRESS language and the EXPRESS-G representation will be introduced in detail in the following section.

3.2 The EXPRESS language

The EXPRESS language [ISO94b] is an international standard (ISO 10303-11). It is a formal information model specification language.

The EXPRESS language is readable to humans and fully computer interpretable. It was originally developed within the context of the **ST**andard for the **E**xchange of **P**roduct Model Data (STEP) [ISO94a], but is currently used for many other purposes, including applications outside STEP.

EXPRESS-G [ISO94] provides a graphical notation for a subset of the EXPRESS language constructs. It is intended for human communication. In the following introduction to EXPRESS, the corresponding EXPRESS-G symbols will be presented too.

In this section, an example will be used to illustrate schemas, entities, attributes, and generalization/specialization relationships in EXPRESS. This example model is the point concept in the geometrical domain. A point has an x-coordinate, a y-coordinate and an optional z-coordinate. A coordinate can be relative or absolute, and it has a coordinate value attribute. A length can be specified using three units: metres, centimetres and millimetres, with millimetres as the default. The example model will be described in both the textual form of EXPRESS and the EXPRESS-G graphical form (See Figure 3.1). The detail of the EXPRESS language and the corresponding symbols in EXPRESS-G are introduced in the following sections.

```
SCHEMA pointModel;


TYPE value = REAL;
WHERE
        notLessThanZero : SELF >= 0.0;
END_TYPE;


ENTITY point;
x: coordinate;
        y: coordinate;
        z: OPTIONAL coordinate;
END_ENTITY;


ENTITY coordinate;
        ABSTRACT SUPERTYPE OF (ONEOF (absoluteCoordinate,
                                        relativeCoordinate));
        coordinateValue : length;
INVERSE
        containingPointX : SET [0:1] OF point FOR x;
        containingPoinyY : SET [0:1] OF point FOR y;
        containingPointZ : SET [0:1] OF point FOR z;
containingRelativeCoordinate : SET [0:1] OF relativeCoordinate FOR
lastCoordinate;
WHERE
        validExistence :SIZEOF(containingPointX)+
                        SIZEOF(containingPointY)+
                        SIZEOF(containingPointZ)+
```

```
                              SIZEOF(containingRelativeCoordinate) = 1;
END_ENTITY;


ENTITY absoluteCoordinate;
      SUBTYPE OF (coordinate);
END_ENTITY;


ENTITY relativeCoordinate;
      SUBTYPE OF (coordinate);
      lastCoordinate : coordinate;
END_ENTITY;


ENTITY length
      ABSTRACT SUPERTYPE OF(ONEOF (lengthInMetres,
                                  lengthInCentimetres,
                                  lengthInMillimetres));
      lengthValueInMillimetres : value;
INVERSE
containingCoordinate : coordinate FOR coordinateValue;
END_ENTITY;


ENTITY lengthInMetres
      SUBTYPE OF(length);
      lengthValueInMetres : value;
DERIVE
SELF\length.lengthValueInMillimetres : value :=
lengthValueInMetres*1000;
END_ENTITY;


ENTITY lengthInCentimetres
      SUBTYPE OF(length);
      lengthValueInCentiMetres : value;
DERIVE
      SELF\length.lengthValueInMillimetres : value :=
lengthValueInCentiMetres*10;
END_ENTITY;


ENTITY lengthInMillimetres
      SUBTYPE OF(length);
END_ENTITY;
```

```
END_SCHEMA;
```

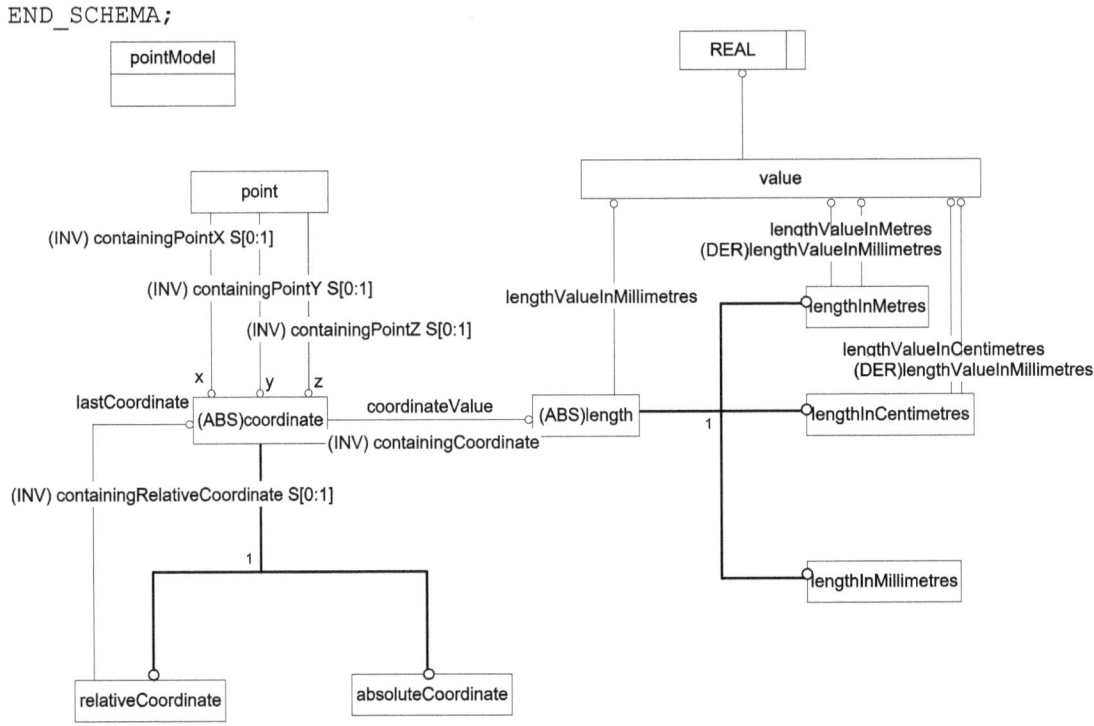

Figure 3.1 The PointModel Schema in EXPRESS-G

3.2.1 SCHEMA

In EXPRESS, a schema is a wrapper for a collection of related information. It is used to encompass the objects, relationships and constraints for a particular universe of functionality. In other words, the contents in a given schema must all describe a common domain. A schema is defined by a pair of tags, the head one is SCHEMA, followed by identification, and the tail one is END_SCHEMA. Between them is the schema body, which consists of some declarations. In the above example, there is one schema, pointModel. In Figure 3.1, the pointModel schema in EXPRESS-G is described by a rectangle with the identification enclosed in it. The identification is above a horizontal line that is in the centre of the rectangle.

The order in which objects are declared is not relevant to the meaning of a schema as a whole or to the individual things declared within it. There must be well-defined limits to a given schema. It cannot describe everything, but should be constrained to fit the domain intended. A single schema cannot sensibly be used to describe two or more different domains.

An EXPRESS information model may include one or more schemas, but the schema definitions may not be nested. A schema can, however, draw from declarations made in other schemas. There are two interface specifications (USE and REFERENCE), both of which enable items to become visible. The USE specification allows items declared in one schema to be independently instantiated in the schema specifying the USE construct, whereas the items that are explicitly referenced by a REFERENCE construct can only be instantiated to play the role described by an attribute of an instantiation of an entity in the schema.

3.2.2 Data types

This section introduces the data types provided as part of the EXPRESS language. Every attribute, local variable or formal parameter has an associated data type. The data types in EXPRESS can be classified as simple data types, aggregation data types, named data types, constructed data types and generalized data types. They are shown in Figure 3.2.

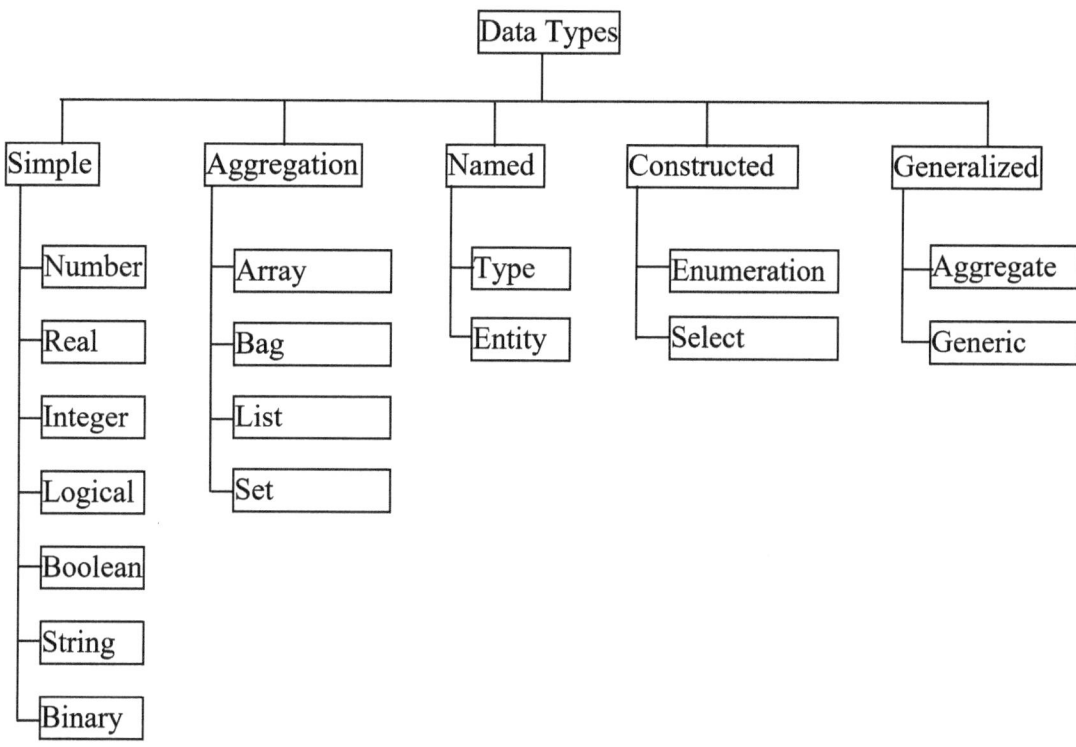

Figure 3.2 Data Types in EXPRESS

3.2.2.1 Simple data type

The simple data types define the domain of the atomic units in EXPRESS. That is they cannot be further subdivided into elements that EXPRESS recognizes. The simple data types are NUMBER, REAL, BINARY, INTEGER, LOGICAL, BOOLEAN and STRING [ISO94b]. Figure 3.3 illustrates the symbols used for simple data types in EXPRESS-G. A simple data type is denoted by a rectangular solid box with a double vertical line at the right end of the box. The name of the data type is enclosed within the box.

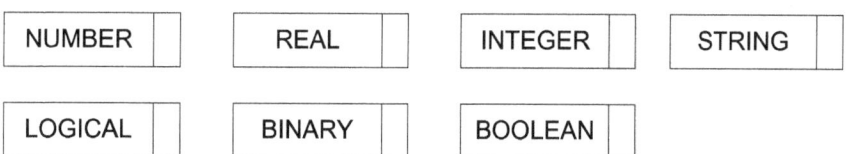

Figure 3.3 Basic Data Types in EXPRESS-G

In Figure 3.1, the simple data type REAL is used to define the value named data type.

3.2.2.2 Aggregation data type

Aggregation data types have as their domain collections of values of a given base data type. These base data type values are called elements of the aggregation collection. There are four kinds of aggregation data type: BAG, SET, LIST and ARRAY. Each kind of aggregation data type attaches different properties to its values [ISO94b]. The four sorts of aggregation data type differ in three aspects: the size specification variability, the indexing/ordering of elements and element occurrence. This is shown in Table 3.3.

The declaration of an aggregation data type consists of aggregation data identification, an optional boundary specification and base type identification. In the pointModel schema, all the INVERSE attributes of the coordinate entity are assigned the SET aggregation data type.

Aggregation Type	Size	Index/order	Element occurrence
ARRAY	Fixed	Indexed	Multiple/unique
LIST	Variable	Ordered	Multiple/unique
SET	Variable	Unordered	Unique
BAG	Variable	Unordered	Multiple

Table 3.3 Aggregation Data Types in EXPRESS

3.2.2.3 Named data type

The named data types are the data types that may be declared in a formal specification. There are two kinds of named data type: the `entity` data type and the defined data types.

`Entity` data types are established by entity declarations. The `entity` data type is introduced in Section 3.2.3.

A defined data type is created based on another type (the underlying type). The `value` data type in the `pointModel` schema is an example of a defined data type; it is created based on the REAL simple data type. The semantics of a defined data type is greater than its underlying type. A defined data type can be used to distinguish conceptually different collections of values that happen to have similar representations. With the help of defined data types, the maintainability of the model is increased.

In EXPRESS, a named data type is defined by a pair of tags. The head tag is `TYPE,` followed by identification and the underlying data type. The tail tag is `END_TYPE`. In EXPRESS-G, the symbol for a named data type consists of a dashed box enclosing its name. In Figure 3.1, the defined data type named `value` is a good case in point.

3.2.2.4 Constructed data type

There are two kinds of constructed data types in EXPRESS: ENUMERATION data types and SELECT data types, described in Table 3.4. These data types have similar syntactic structures and are used to provide the underlying representation of defined data types.

Constructed data type	Description
ENUMERATION data type	This defines an ordered set of names. It is used to make data available as a set of static values.
SELECT data type	This makes defined data types available as a grouped set of named data types.

Table 3.4 Constructed Data Types in EXPRESS

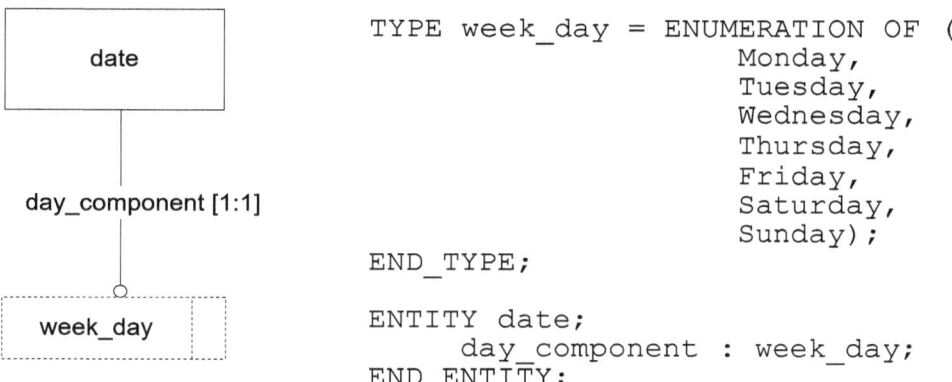

```
TYPE week_day = ENUMERATION OF (
                    Monday,
                    Tuesday,
                    Wednesday,
                    Thursday,
                    Friday,
                    Saturday,
                    Sunday);
END_TYPE;

ENTITY date;
    day_component : week_day;
END_ENTITY;
```

Figure 3.4 The Week_day Enumeration Data Type in EXPRESS-G and EXPRESS

In EXPRESS, a constructed data type is defined by a pair of tags. The head tag is `TYPE`, followed by its identification and the constructed data type, `ENUMERATION` or `SELECT`. The tail tag is `END_TYPE`. Between them is a list of the basic elements. In EXPRESS-G, the symbol for a constructed data type consists of a dashed box enclosing its name, with double lines at one end. The `ENUMERATION` has the double lines at the right end, whereas the `SELECT` has the double lines at the left end. Figure 3.4 is an example of the `ENUMERATION` data type. The `week_day` is an enumeration of all weekdays, and the `day_component` attribute of the `date` entity receives values of this `ENUMERATION` data type.

3.2.2.5 Generalized data type

The generalized data types are used to specify a generalization of other data types, and can only be used in certain contexts. The `GENERIC` type is a generalization of all data types. The `AGGREGATE` data type is a generalization of all aggregation data types. Both of them can only be used as the types of the formal parameters of functions and procedures.

```
FUNCTION scale (in:AGGREGATE OF INTEGER, scalar:NUMBER) : AGGREGATE
OF INTEGER;

LOCAL

    Result:AGGREGATE OF INTEGER := [];

END_LOCAL;

REPEAT i:= LOINDEX(in) TO HIINDEX(in);

    Result[i] := scalar *in[i];

END_REPEAT;

RETURN (result);

END_FUNCTION;
```

There is a `scale` function in the above excerpt of an information model in EXPRESS. The data type of the `in` formal parameter is AGGREGATE, which means the actual parameter can be a `BAG`, `SET`, `ARRAY` or `LIST`.

3.2.3 ENTITY

An entity represents an object of interest in the universe of discourse. In other words, it is a class of information, which represents conceptual or real world objects that have common properties. In the `pointModel` example, there are eight entities: `point`, `coordinate`, `absoluteCoordinate`, `length`, `lengthInMetres`, `lengthInCentimetres` and `lengthInMillimetres`.

An entity can also play the role of a data type. In the `pointModel` schema in Figure 3.1, the `length` entity is the data type of the values that the `coordinateValue` attribute of the `coordinate` entity may receive. In addition, the `length` entity holds additional semantics and means more than a data type; it means the length in that model. Therefore, an entity represents a real world object, which may work as a data type too.

In EXPRESS, an entity is declared by a pair of tags; the head tag is `ENTITY`, followed by identification, the tail tag is `END_ENTITY`. Between them is the body of the `entity`, which consists of some `attributes` and `constraints`.

EXPRESS-G uses the solid box symbol for `ENTITY` definition. The name of the entity is enclosed by the box. In Figure 3.1, the `point` entity is an example.

3.2.4 Attributes

An attribute is a characteristic, quality or property of an entity. It can be qualified by various additional specifiers, such as `OPTIONAL`, `UNIQUE`, `DERIVE` and `INVERSE`.

It is not always necessary to specify values for all attributes defined in an entity. Where it is not always assigned a value, an attribute may be marked as `OPTIONAL`. An optional attribute that happens not to have an explicitly assigned value is given the value indeterminate (?). For example, the z attribute of the `point` entity (See Figure 3.1) is not mandatory, because the z-coordinate is not mandatory for a 2D point. Therefore, the z attribute is marked `OPTIONAL`.

The `UNIQUE` keyword is used in two different contexts. The first context is that `UNIQUE` can be associated with an aggregation attribute definition. For example, a list of members of a group might be defined as:

group_members : LIST [0:?] OF UNIQUE member;

In this statement, `UNIQUE` means that all members of the `LIST` must be different from each other.

The `UNIQUE` keyword can also be used to specify a form of rule that applies to all occurrences of the current entity type in a representation of the Universe of Discourse.

An attribute declared in a supertype can be redeclared in its subtypes. In the `2D-point` example, the `lengthValueInMillimetres` of supertype `length` is redeclared in its subtypes `lengthInMetres` and `lengthInCentimetres`, because it should be calculated from the other private attributes of the subtypes.

The use of `INVERSE` makes the attribute dependency relationship explicit for certain cases. It is used, in the context of this thesis, to specify existence dependency between an entity and the use of that entity. For example, the `point` entity uses `coordinate` entity to define the data types of its attributes such as x and y, so the existence of the `coordinate` entity is dependent on the `point` entity.

In EXPRESS-G, an attribute of an entity is described by a line between the entity and the data types of the values of the attribute. On the line end that connects the symbol of the data types of the values, there is a little circle. The identification and some other specifiers of the attribute are placed on the line.

3.2.5 Generalization/specialization

The EXPRESS language uses a `supertype/subtype` mechanism to represent the generalization/specialization relationship.

A `subtype` entity is more specific than its `supertypes`, and a `supertype` entity is more general than its `subtypes`. A `subtype` entity inherits all of the properties of its `supertypes`, including attributes and constraints. For example, the `coordinate` entity is a `supertype` and has two subtypes, `absoluteCoordinate` and `relativeCoordinate`. Coordinates are general and can be classified to be absolute coordinates or relative ones. The `coordinateValue` attribute will be inherited by the `subtypes`.

A `subtype` entity may have more than one `supertype`, because the EXPRESS language supports multiple-inheritance.

In EXPRESS-G, the entities forming an inheritance graph are connected by thick solid lines. The circled end of the relationship line denotes the subtype end of the relationship. When a `supertype` is abstract, the characters ABS, enclosed by parentheses, precede the name of the entity within the entity symbol box.

3.2.6 Constraints

In addition to the data types and their relationships, the EXPRESS language also supports the declarations of some constraints.

When defining data types or the relationships between them, it is always necessary to insert some assertions on the domain of valid values. For example, the `value` data type has a local rule `notLessThanZero`. Such a constraint asserts all values in `value` must be greater zero.

There are twelve sorts of constraints in the EXPRESS language. They are listed in Table 3.5.

No.	*Constraint Types*
1	Aggregation datatype (used in attribute declaration) bound specification
2	`UNIQUE` reserved word in attribute declarations (Uniqueness rules)
3	`OPTIONAL` reserved word in attribute declarations
4	`WHERE` rules applied on attributes (Domain rules)
5	`RULE` structures
6	Abstract supertype entity
7	Subtype constraint
8	`WHERE` rules applied on defined datatypes
9	`DERIVE` reserved word (attribute derivation)
10	Attribute redeclaration in subtype entities
11	`UNIQUE` reserved word in aggregation datatype declarations
12	`INVERSE` reserved word (inverse attribute)

Table 3.5 Constraint Types in EXPRESS

3.2.6.1 Aggregation data type bound specification

Pattern 1 in Table 3.5 is the aggregation datatype bound specification. It specifies the minimum and maximum number of elements that can be held in the collection defined by the aggregation datatype. The `containingPointX` attribute in the `coordinate` entity has a set as its underlying data type. The bound specification of that set type is `[0:1]`, which states that the set should have at most one element, and can be empty.

3.2.6.2 `UNIQUE` reserved word in attribute declaration (Uniqueness rule)

Pattern 2 in Table 3.5 is the `UNIQUE` reserved word in attribute declaration. In the EXPRESS manual it is also called a uniqueness rule. It specifies that no two instances of an entity datatype in the model shall have the same value for the named attribute.

3.2.6.3 `OPTIONAL` reserved word in attributes

Pattern 3 in Table 3.5 is the `OPTIONAL` reserved word. It indicates that, in a given entity instance, the attribute need not have a value. If the attribute has no value, the value is said to be indeterminate. The `z` attribute in the `point` entity is an example of this pattern. It means that the z coordinate is not compulsory for a point.

3.2.6.4 WHERE rules applied on attributes

Pattern 4 in Table 3.5 is the WHERE rule applied on attributes. WHERE rules in entities are also called domain rules. A domain rule constrains the values of individual attributes or combinations of attributes for every entity instance. The `validExistence` domain rule in the `coordinate` entity illustrates this constraint pattern.

3.2.6.5 RULE structures

Pattern 5 in Table 3.5 is the RULE construct in the EXPRESS language. RULEs permit the definition of constraints that apply to one or more entity data types within the scope of a schema. A RULE declaration permits the definition of constraints that apply collectively to the entire population of an entity, or to instances of more than one entity data type, whereas the local rules such as the UNIQUE reserved word and domain rules in an entity declaration declare constraints that apply individually to every instance of an entity.

3.2.6.6 Abstract supertype entity

Pattern 6 in Table 3.5 is the ABSTRACT declaration of a supertype entity. It specifies that the entity which is declared to be ABSTRACT can only be instantiated through its subtypes. The `coordinate` entity is abstract, so it can only be instantiated through its subtype entities: `absoluteCoordinate` and `relativeCoordinate`.

3.2.6.7 Subtype constraint

Pattern 7 in Table 3.5 is a subtype constraint. An instance of a subtype entity is an instance of each of its supertypes. An instance of an entity that is either explicitly or implicitly declared to be a supertype may also be an instance of one or more of its subtypes. This pattern specifies the constraints on which subtype/supertype graphs may be instantiated. There are three sorts of subtype constraints: ONEOF, ANDOR and AND. The ONEOF constraint is used in declaring the inheritance relationship between the `coordinate` entity and its subtypes: `absoluteCoordinate` and `relativeCoordinate`. It specifies that the subtypes of the `coordinate` entity, the `absoluteCoordinate` entity and the `relativeCoordinate` entity are mutually exclusive.

3.2.6.8 WHERE rules applied on defined data types

Pattern 8 in Table 3.5 is a WHERE rule applied on defined data types. A WHERE rule applied on a defined data type specifies a constraint that restricts the domain of the defined data type. This pattern is called a domain rule as well (see Pattern 4). The domain of a defined data type is the domain of its underlying representation constrained by the domain rules. The `notLessThanZero` constraint in the `value` type is an example of this pattern. It specifies that `value` shall not be less than zero.

3.2.6.9 DERIVE reserved word (attribute derivation)

Pattern 9 in Table 3.5 is the DERIVE reserved word, which stands for attribute derivation. A derived attribute represents a property whose value is computed by evaluating an expression. In the `lengthInMetres` entity, the `lengthValueInMillimetres` is a derived attribute. The value of the `lengthValueInMillimetres` attribute is computed by evaluating an expression: `lengthValueInMetres*1000`.

3.2.6.10 Attribute redeclaration

Pattern 10 in Table 3.5 is attribute redeclaration. An attribute declared in a supertype can be redeclared in a subtype. The attribute remains in the supertype but the allowed domain of values for that attribute is governed by the redeclaration given in the subtype.

3.2.6.11 UNIQUE reserved word in aggregation declaration

Pattern 11 in Table 3.5 is the UNIQUE reserved word in an aggregation datatype declaration. It specifies a constraint that all elements in an aggregation datatype shall be different.

3.2.6.12 INVERSE reserved word (inverse attribute)

Pattern 12 in Table 3.5 is the INVERSE reserved word. If another entity has established a relationship with the current entity by way of an explicit attribute, an inverse attribute may be used to describe that relationship in the context of the current entity. An inverse attribute declaration also names an explicit attribute of the referencing entity. For a particular instance of the current entity, the value of the inverse attribute consists of the instance or instances of the referencing entity which use the current instance in the role specified. The containingPointY attribute in the coordinate entity is an inverse attribute. It specifies that the value of the containingPointY attribute shall be the instance of the point entity that refers to the current instance of the coordinate entity as the value of its y attribute.

3.3 EXPRESS model based software engineering

Generally, the application domains of EXPRESS have been electronic design and manufacture related. Current application areas include the management of electronic design and manufacturing processes and the system-level design of electronic based projects. Two software engineering techniques underpin this work: the use of EXPRESS models to describe domains and the use of these models as specifications from which implementations are generated.

It is developing a software infrastructure that includes tools to exploit EXPRESS information models to provide an environment to transform models, to generate implementations of those models and to process instance data that conforms to those models. Figure 3.5 illustrates the overall infrastructure.

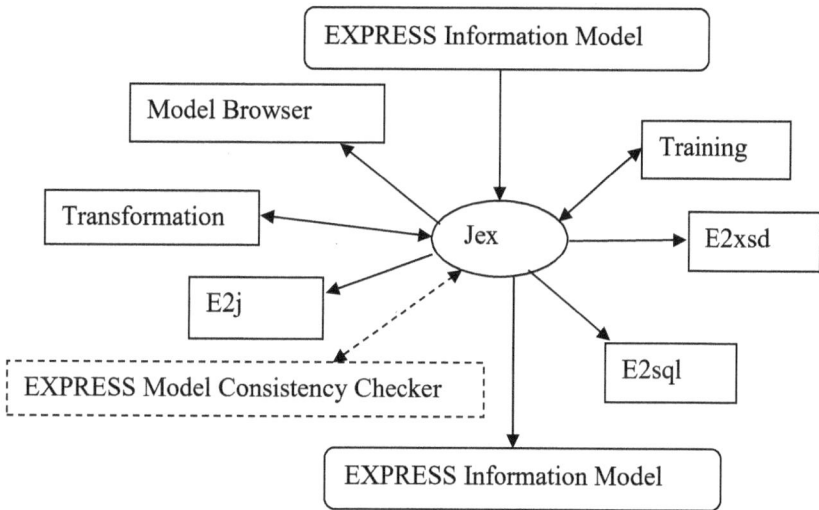

Figure 3.5 Infrastructure of EXPRESS-Model-Based Software Environment

Using this infrastructure, it is possible to read an input EXPRESS model into memory and build an in-memory representation using Jex [MINT], which is a Java Application Interface (API) and a software library implementation of that API for manipulating EXPRESS models. Other tools such as E2xsd, E2sql and E2j [MINT] then read the in-memory representation and produce some other representations of the input EXPRESS model. The representations can be XML schemas, SQL code and Java classes.

The input to this infrastructure, EXPRESS models, is the root of all other representations generated using the EXPRESS tools in the infrastructure. All model representations are dependent on the input model. Hence, it is very important to guarantee the correctness of the EXPRESS models that are to be manipulated by the infrastructure.

3.4 Consistency issues in EXPRESS models

There are various consistency issues in EXRESS models, just as there were in the languages introduced in Chapter 2. The following EXPRESS model contains a trivial example of inconsistency.

```
SCHEMA personModel;
ENTITY person;
    howOld: age;
```

```
WHERE
        r1: SELF.howOld < 0;
END_ENTITY;

TYPE age = INTEGER;
WHERE
naturalNumber: SELF >= 0;
END_TYPE;
END_SCHEMA;
```

The `personModel` schema is syntactically correct and passes through EXPRESS syntax checkers. However, this model is not semantically correct. In the `personModel` schema, the `age` defined data type, whose underlying data type is `INTEGER`, is actually constrained to be a natural number. Whereas the `person` entity references the `age` data type to its `howOld` attribute and constrains it to be less than zero. All EXPRESS modellers would agree that there is a logical contradiction between the `naturalNumber` constraint in the `age` defined data type and the `r1` constraint applied on the `howOld` attribute in the `person` entity. The `age` defined data type is referenced by the `howOld` attribute in the `person` entity, but it cannot provide any value that meets both the `r1` and the `naturalNumber` constraints. Such a logical contradiction makes the `person` entity inconsistent and prevents the `personModel` schema from being correct and useful.

Inconsistent models may be correct, viewed from the perspective of syntax, but they do not match any possible and reasonable target systems. In other words, inconsistent information models are paradoxes.

3.4.1 Characteristics of inconsistency in EXPRESS models

An EXPRESS model consists of data types (including entity types) and some constraints applied to those data types. The data types build the skeleton of an EXPRESS model, while the constraints further describe the detail and characteristics of the corresponding data types.

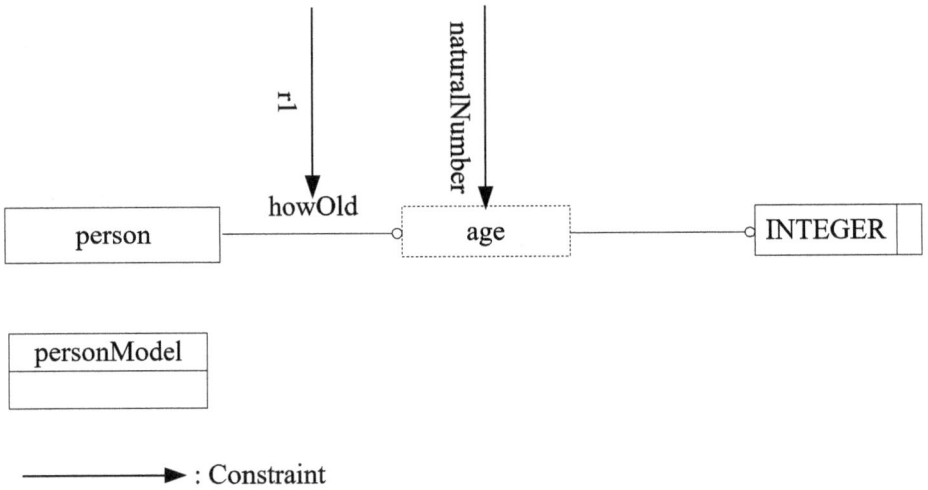

Figure 3.6 The PersonModel

For example, in the `personModel` schema, which is illustrated in Figure 3.6, there are three data types: the `person` entity type, the `age` defined data type and the `INTEGER` built-in data type. The `INTEGER` built-in data type has a role as the underlying type of the user defined data type `age`, and the latter is the data type of the `howOld` attribute in the `person` entity. These data types build the skeleton of the `personModel`.

Figure 3.6 also illustrates two constraints in the `personModel` schema; these are identified as `r1` and `naturalNumber`. These constraints, built on the base of the datatypes, provide more information and characterise the model in a richer way.

3.4.1.1 Inconsistency: conflicts among constraints

Inconsistencies in an EXPRESS model are the contradictions among the constraints. Such contradictions make the constraints fail to be satisfiable together. In the `personModel` schema, the

```
r1: SELF.howOld < 0;
```

and the

```
naturalNumber: SELF >= 0;
```

constraints conflict with each other and cannot be satisfied concurrently.

A new model, `SimplifiedPersonModel`, is a simplified version of `personModel`. The constraints are removed.

```
SCHEMA SimplifiedPersonModel;
ENTITY person;
     howOld : age;
END_ENTITY;
TYPE age = INTEGER;
END_TYPE;
END_SCHEMA;
```

The `SimplifiedPersonModel` becomes consistent, because those inconsistent constraints are removed.

This conclusion also leads to a hint for identifying inconsistency or proving consistency.

3.4.1.2 Inconsistency: invalid data types

A consistent model implies that all of the model constraints have at least one common solution, i.e. there is at least one instance of the model and all EXPRESS constructs in the model, such as the entities, data types, relationships and constraints, that can be instantiated or be logically true together.

On the other hand, inconsistency causes one or more of the data types (including entity data types) to be unable to contain any values, and hence to be invalid.

For example, the `age` defined data type in `personModel` is valid, because it states some values, such as 5 and 17 that meet the `naturalNumber` constraint. However, the anonymous data type of the `howOld` attribute is not valid, because there is no value that meets the requirement of `r1` and `naturalNumber` concurrently. Failure of the `howOld` attribute further leads to the invalidity of the `person` entity data type.

Consistency of an EXPRESS model can be represented as the validity of the data types in it. This conclusion provides another clue to EXPRESS model consistency checking.

3.4.2 Inconsistency patterns

Section 3.4.1.1 argues that an inconsistency is the result of constraints conflicting with each other. Different kinds of constraints meeting and conflicting produce a variety of inconsistency patterns. For example, the inconsistency in the `personModel` falls into a pattern that may be defined as the conflict between a local rule (`r1`) in an entity type and a domain rule (`naturalNumber`) in a defined data type.

Section 3.2.6 identifies twelve sorts of constraints in the EXPRESS language. Appendix 1 lists twenty inconsistency patterns based on just two constraints intersecting and conflicting with each other.

However, the patterns of inconsistencies in the EXPRESS language are infinite, because clearly more than two constraints can exist that reference the same object and conflict with each other. For example, the following shows an inconsistency among three local rules.

```
ENTITY 3_input_gate;
      input_1: BOOLEAN;
      input_2: BOOLEAN;
      input_3: BOOLEAN;
WHERE
      rule_1: input_1 OR input_2 = FALSE;
      rule_2: input_1 OR input_3 = FALSE;
      rule_3: input_3 OR input_2 = TRUE;
END_ENTITY;
```

In the 3_input_gate entity, there are three attributes: input_1, input_2 and input_3. Their underlying data types are BOOLEAN. There are three constraints in the 3_input_gate entity: rule_1, rule_2 and rule_3. The 3_input_gate entity is not consistent, and the inconsistency is among the three WHERE rules. This inconsistency does not fall into the patterns listed in Appendix 1. Infinite numbers of inconsistency patterns may exist and hence it is not feasible to identify all possible patterns.

3.4.3 Static/Dynamic Inconsistencies

Chapter 1 introduces the idea that inconsistencies can be classified as static and dynamic ones. EXPRESS models concentrate on describing the static structure of the objects in a domain; therefore most inconsistencies in EXPRESS models are static. For example, the 3_input_gate entity in Section 3.4.2 describes the static property of a gate which has three inputs, and the inconsistency among the WHERE rules is static.

However, the RULE structure, which was introduced in Section 3.2.6.5, brings dynamic activities into EXPRESS models. Because a RULE declaration permits the definition of constraints that apply collectively to the entire population of an entity, or to instances of more than one entity data type, it implies some dynamic information such as instantiation. Moreover, the body of a RULE may have executable statements such as value assignment and loop, which can be regarded as dynamic transformation of an object. Therefore the RULE structure related inconsistencies are dynamic.

Consider the example in inconsistency pattern 7, Appendix 1.

```
SCHEMA rule2WHERE;
ENTITY a;
      b : INTEGER;
WHERE
      w1 : SELF.b >= 5;
END_ENTITY;


RULE r1 FOR (a);
LOCAL
      temp : SET OF a := [];
END_LOCAL;
      temp := QUERY (temp < * a | temp.b < 5);
WHERE
      w1 : SIZEOF (temp) > =1;
```

```
END_RULE;

END_SCHEMA;
```

In `r1`, the `temp` variable is instantiated to be an empty set, and then contains some instances of the `a` entity which go through the `QUERY` operation. `r1` describes two snapshots of the target system: instantiation of `temp`, and assigning the `QUERY` result to `temp`. The inconsistency between these two snapshots is dynamic.

3.5 Summary

Information modelling and its applications is the main topic of this chapter. The EXPRESS language supports the declaration of entities, data types and a variety of constraints.

However, EXPRESS models may contain consistency issues just as other languages do. Inconsistencies are caused by the conflicts among constraints. Sixteen inconsistency patterns have been identified. Most inconsistencies in EXPRESS models are static, but the `RULE` related inconsistencies are dynamic. The characteristics and classification of inconsistencies in EXPRESS models provide some hints to solving these issues.

4 Checking EXPRESS models for consistency

After consistency issues in EXPRESS models were introduced in Chapter 3, this chapter moves the focus onto addressing consistency issues in EXPRESS models.

Chapter 2 analysed consistency at the semantic level from a theoretical standpoint and introduced issues relating to addressing consistency in a variety of languages, such as UML, OWL and CP. When studying checking EXPRESS model consistency, it is therefore reasonable and necessary to exploit the conclusions drawn in Chapter 2 and to consider the feasibility of applying the consistency checking technologies studied in Chapter 2 to the EXPRESS models. Four approaches had been considered during the research on EXPRESS model consistency checking. After analysis and comparison, the approach that is based on CP was adopted.

This chapter then concentrates on checking EXPRESS model consistency by using CP. That approach is actually a procedure that involves the extraction and solution of the complete and non-redundant Constraint Satisfaction Problems (CSPs) from the EXPRESS model. EXPRESS model formalization and result export, which are helpful to consistency checking, will be introduced as well.

The research introduced in this book not only identified CP for the purpose of EXPRESS model consistency checking and worked out the checking procedure, but also formally described that procedure in a model based manner. That model-based consistency checking activity is also briefly described in this chapter. In order to introduce the formal and model based description of consistency checking, some related modelling technologies such as model mapping in the EXPRESS-X language [ISO99] are also introduced in this chapter.

4.1 Review of the EXPRESS language: Syntax, Semantics and Formalism

The EXPRESS language, which has been introduced in Section 3.2, is an informal language. It has a well-defined syntax in Wirth Syntax Notation [Wirth]. Annex A in the official EXPRESS reference manual [ISO94b] defines the lexical elements of the EXPRESS language and the grammar rules to which these elements must conform.

The EXPRESS language is distinguished by its expressive power (See Section 3.2) and being relatively easy to learn and use. Its definition has been initially motivated by the need for the computer-interpretable representation and exchange of product data. The following table represents the initial design goals of the EXPRESS language.

	Design Goals
1	Parsable by both computers and humans;
2	Enable partitioning of the diverse material addressed by ISO 10303;
3	Support definition of entities, which represent objects of interest;
4	Avoid specific implementation views.

Table 4.1 Design Goal of the EXPRESS Language

Table 4.1 lists four objectives of the EXPRESS language; none of them mentions validation and verification, although verification and validation later became an important aspect. The main focus when defining the EXPRESS language was essentially on entity, attribute and data type definition rather than on the creation of a strictly formal foundation for the language and its models. Moreover, although the STEP community has attempted to address validation and verification of models, it has not exploited the kinds of formal approach, which are the key methods in formal design and verification.

Semantics, which was introduced in Section 2.1.2, is concerned with the meaning of phrases in a language [Watt]. Formal semantics, as described in Section 2.1.3, is concerned with rigorously specifying meaning or behaviour. The need for rigour arises because it can reveal ambiguities and subtle complexities in apparently crystal clear defining documents and can form the basis for analysis and verification [Nielson]. The EXPRESS language has not got well-defined formal semantics. For example, in the EXPRESS language, a data type is regarded as a domain of values, and an entity is regarded as a class of information defined by common properties (Section 3.2 in [ISO94b]). Those definitions of data types and entities are based on common sense knowledge and concepts, not mathematics. This sort of semantics of the EXPRESS language is sufficient for reading and understanding, but not sufficient for reasoning and proof. In brief the EXPRESS language has a well-defined syntax in Wirth Syntax Notation, but its semantics is informal.

4.2 Identifying an appropriate approach for EXPRESS model consistency checking

Proof reading by domain experts has been until now the only approach available to check the kinds of EXPRESS model consistency issues introduced in Chapter 3. The research objective here is to see if it is possible to develop a standard and formal consistency checking approach, which is domain independent and applicable to all EXPRESS models. Four approaches, illustrated in Figure 4.1 have been recognized and compared, and the most capable one is identified for further study, implementation and test.

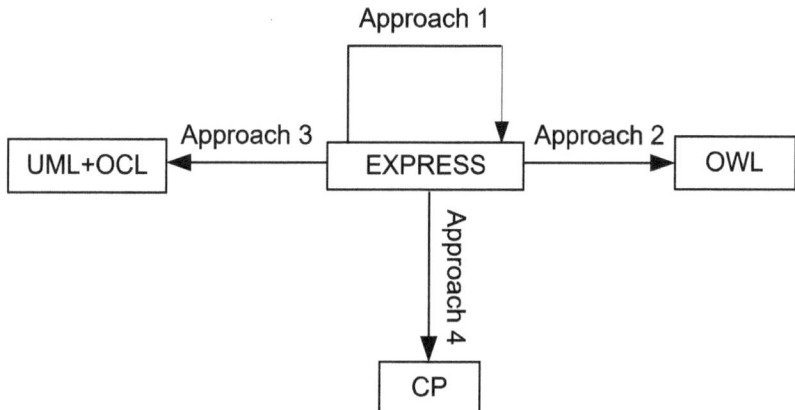

Figure 4.1 The Recognized Approaches to EXPRESS Model Consistency Checking

4.2.1 Approach 1

The first recognized approach in Figure 4.1 is to identify all inconsistency patterns in EXPRESS models and then find a solution to each of them. No theories and methods that are out of the domain of the EXPRESS language would be used. The following practical models had been studied in order to identify the patterns and properties of possible inconsistencies.

- The model of the Gerber format [Gerber] (The Gerber model);
- The Jex model [Mint];
- The model of the Scalable Vector Graphics (SVG) [W3Ce];
- The model of ISO 10303-41 [ISO91a];
- The model of ISO 10303-43 [ISO91b];
- The model of Computer Aided Design (**CAD**) Framework Interface and Design Representation (**CFIDR**) [CFI].

Some inconsistency patterns had been identified from those models, which were introduced in Section 3.4.2.

However, it was later found that this approach was infeasible. First, it is impossible to identify all inconsistency patterns in EXPRESS models, because the inconsistency patterns are infinite (see Section 3.4.2). Second, the informal semantics of the EXPRESS language does not provide a sufficiently rigid platform on which consistency checking that involves reasoning and proof can run.

Although the first approach to EXPRES model consistency checking failed, some helpful lessons were learned:

- It is impossible to address the consistency issues without the help from the other Computer Science theories or methods.
- Formal semantics is necessary for consistency checking.

4.2.2 Approach 2: OWL

The second recognized approach to EXPRESS model consistency checking is to make use of the consistency checking ability in OWL. As introduced in Section 2.2.2, OWL has a Description Logic semantic, which is decidable, and there are some algorithms and some tools that implement those algorithms which can reason about consistency in OWL specifications.

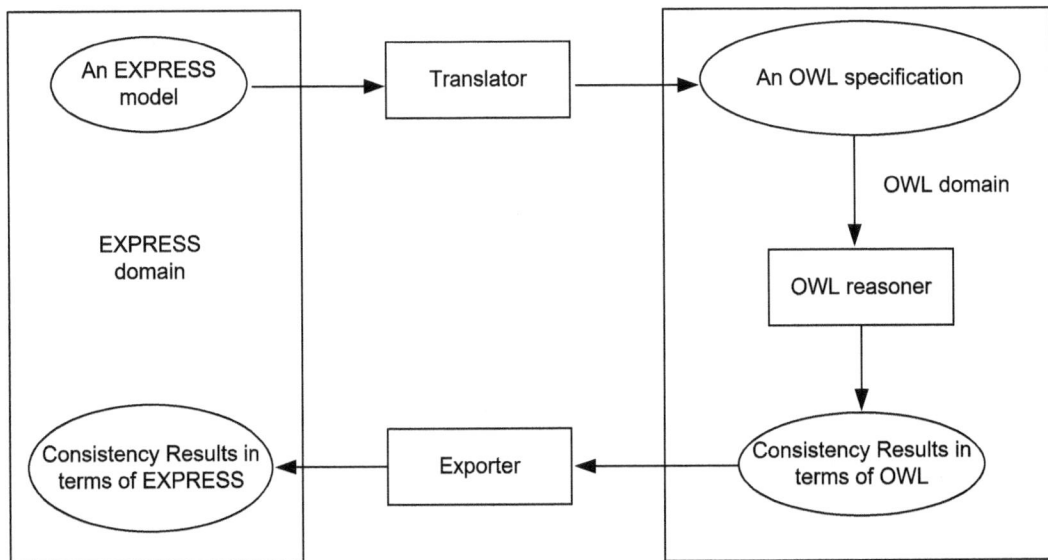

Figure 4.2 Checking EXPRESS Model Consistencies by Using OWL

The initial idea of this approach, illustrated in Figure 4.2, includes translating an EXPRESS model to OWL, reasoning with the OWL specification for consistency, and finally reporting the consistency results in term of EXPRESS. The consistency issues in EXPRESS models transfer to OWL after the EXPRESS models are translated to OWL. In the OWL domain, consistency issues can then be solved with the reasoning tools. For example, the following EXPRESS model, which comes from Section 8, Appendix 1, contains an inconsistency.

```
SCHEMA oneOf2AND;

ENTITY a
     SUPERTYPE OF (ONEOF (b, c));
END_ENTITY;

ENTITY b
     SUBTYPE OF (a);
END_ENTITY;

ENTITY c
     SUBTYPE OF (a);
END_ENTITY;

ENTITY d
     SUBTYPE OF (b,c);
END_ENTITY;

END_SCHEMA;
```

This model can be mapped to OWL.

```
<owl:Class rdf : ID="a">
</owl:Class>

<owl:Class rdf : ID="b">
      <rdfs: subClassOf rdf:resource="#a"/>
</owl:Class>

<owl:Class rdf : ID="c">
      <rdfs: subClassOf rdf:resource="#a"/>
</owl:Class>

<owl:Class rdf : about="#b">
      <owl:disjointWith>
            <owl:Class rdf : about ="#c">
      </owl:disjointWith>
</owl:Class>

<owl:Class rdf: ID="d">
      <rdfs: subClassOf>
            <owl:Class rdf : about ="#b">
      </rdfs:subClassOf>
      <rdfs: subClassOf>
            <owl:Class rdf : about ="#c">
      </rdfs:subClassOf>
</owl:Class>
```

OWL reasoners such as FaCT, can identify that class d in the above OWL specification is uninstantiable. The Exporter, according to this information, can report that entity d in the `oneOf2AND` schema is inconsistent.

However, OWL only matches a limited part of the expressive power of the EXPRESS language, particularly in terms of the constraints that can be described. Some of the EXPRESS language structures and most of the constraints in EXPRESS cannot be mapped to OWL.

OWL does not support the definition and declaration of data types. OWL is a subset of XML and uses the data types in XML Schema [W3Cd] instead of inventing its own data types. Although it is possible to reference data types such as `String`, `Integer` from XML Schema Definition (XSD) [W3Cd], the current Description Logic reasoning algorithms do not support reasoning over data types and values.

OWL does not support the declaration of as many of the constraint patterns as the EXPRESS language does. Table 4.2 shows how many EXPRESS constraints can be represented in OWL. Among twelve EXPRESS constraint patterns, OWL can only represent two; five patterns are out of the scope of the expressiveness of OWL; and five patterns can be partially represented in OWL. Partially represent means that whether an EXPRESS constraint can be mapped to OWL is dependent on its complexity. For example, consider the aggregation data type bound specification in the EXPRESS language, the constraints of this pattern can be partially mapped to OWL. An aggregation data type bound specification in EXPRESS is a numeric expression. If this numeric expression is simple, i.e., only consists of $\leq, \geq$ and $=$, this constraint then can be mapped to OWL. If the numerical expression is complex, i.e., it consists of some other operators such as + and -, this constraint then cannot be mapped to OWL.

No.	*EXPRESS Constraint Types*	*OWL*
1	Aggregation datatype (used in attribute declaration) bound specification	P
2	UNIQUE reserved word in attribute declarations (Uniqueness rules)	N
3	OPTIONAL reserved word in attribute declarations	N
4	WHERE rules applied on attributes (Domain rules)	P

5	`RULE` structures	N
6	Abstract supertype entity	N
7	Subtype constraint	P
8	`WHERE` rules applied on defined datatypes	P
9	`DERIVE` reserved word (attribute derivation)	P
10	Attribute redeclaration in subtype entities	Y
11	`UNIQUE` reserved word in aggregation datatype declarations	N
12	`INVERSE` reserved word (inverse attribute)	Y

Table 4.2 Comparison between EXPRESS Constraints and OWL Constraints

```
Y: OWL can represent this EXPRESS constraint pattern;
N: OWL cannot represent this EXPRESS constraint pattern;
P: OWL can partially represent this EXPRESS constraint pattern.
```

As was stated in Section 3.4.1.1, inconsistencies are conflicts among constraints. Some inconsistencies in EXPRESS models will be missed after the models are translated to OWL, because of the poor expressiveness of OWL.

Therefore, despite the fact that OWL is decidable and that some practical tools such as FaCT exist to support checking consistency in OWL, the idea of mapping EXPRESS models to OWL and then making use of the consistency checking ability in the domain of OWL is not viable.

4.2.3 Approach 3: UML+OCL

The third approach is similar to the second one, making use of the consistency checking tools in the UML+OCL domain. The initial idea of this approach, illustrated in Figure 4.3, includes translating an EXPRESS model to UML+OCL, checking the UML+OCL model for consistency, and finally reporting the consistency results in terms of EXPRESS.

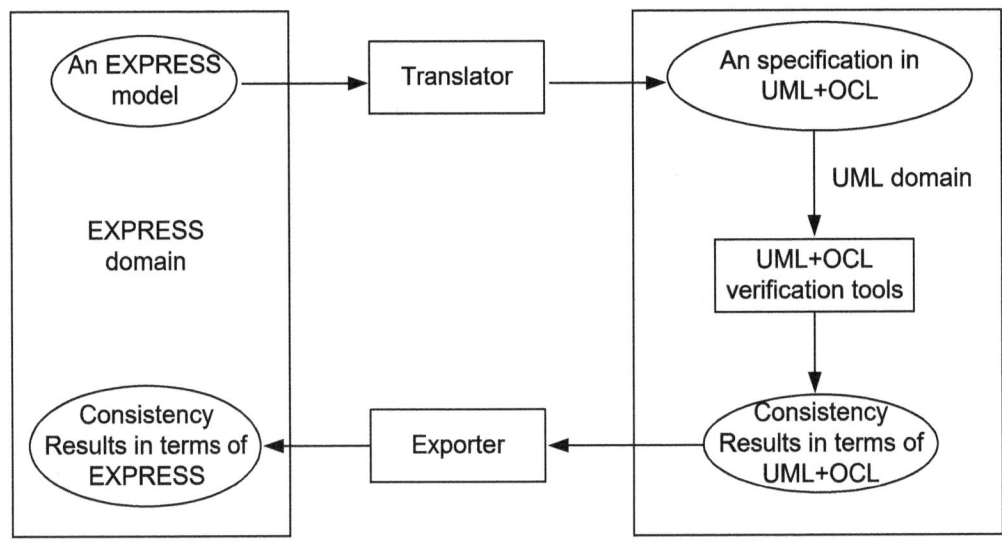

Figure 4.3 Checking EXPRESS Model Consistency with UML+OCL

It was later found that UML+OCL is not suitable for EXPRESS model consistency checking either. UML+OCL is an informal language, similar in that respect to the EXPRESS language. From the perspective of checking consistency, UML+OCL and the EXPRESS language face the same problem. It is helpful to learn from checking UML+OCL models for consistency, but not appropriate to translate the EXPRESS models to UML+OCL for the purpose of consistency checking.

Moreover, UML+OCL only matches a limited part of the expressive power of the EXPRESS language, particularly in terms of the constraints that can be described. Some of the EXPRESS language structures and most of the constraints in EXPRESS cannot be mapped to UML+OCL. Table 4.3 illustrates the comparison between the constraints in EXPRESS and UML+OCL. Among twelve EXPRESS constraint patterns, five can be mapped to UML+OCL, and one type can be partially mapped, but six types cannot be represented in UML+OCL. No UML+OCL checking methods and tools are able to resolve all the possible consistency issues that may occur in EXPRESS models.

No.	*EXPRESS Constraint Types*	*UML+OCL*
1	Aggregation datatype (used in attribute declaration) bound specification	P
2	UNIQUE reserved word in attribute declarations (Uniqueness rules)	N
3	OPTIONAL reserved word in attribute declarations	N
4	WHERE rules applied on attributes (Domain rules)	Y
5	RULE structures	N
6	Abstract supertype entity	Y
7	Subtype constraint	N
8	WHERE rules applied on defined datatypes	N
9	DERIVE reserved word (attribute derivation)	Y
10	Attribute redeclaration in subtype entities	Y
11	UNIQUE reserved word in aggregation datatype declarations	N
12	INVERSE reserved word (inverse attribute)	Y

Table 4.3 Comparison between EXPRESS Constraints and OCL Constraints

```
Y: UML+OCL can represent this EXPRESS constraint pattern;
N: UML+OCL cannot represent this EXPRESS constraint pattern;
P: UML+OCL can partially represent this EXPRESS constraint pattern.
```

4.2.4 Approach 4: CP

The fourth approach is on the basis of Constraint Programming (CP). As it was stated in Section 2.3.4, although CP is not a specification language, consistency issues can be interpreted as CSPs. Checking EXPRESS model consistency can be realized by checking the CSPs extracted from the EXPRESS model for satisfiability. The initial idea of this approach, illustrated in Figure 4.4, includes extracting CSPs from the EXPRESS model, checking the CSPs for satisfiability, and finally exporting the consistency results in terms of EXPRESS.

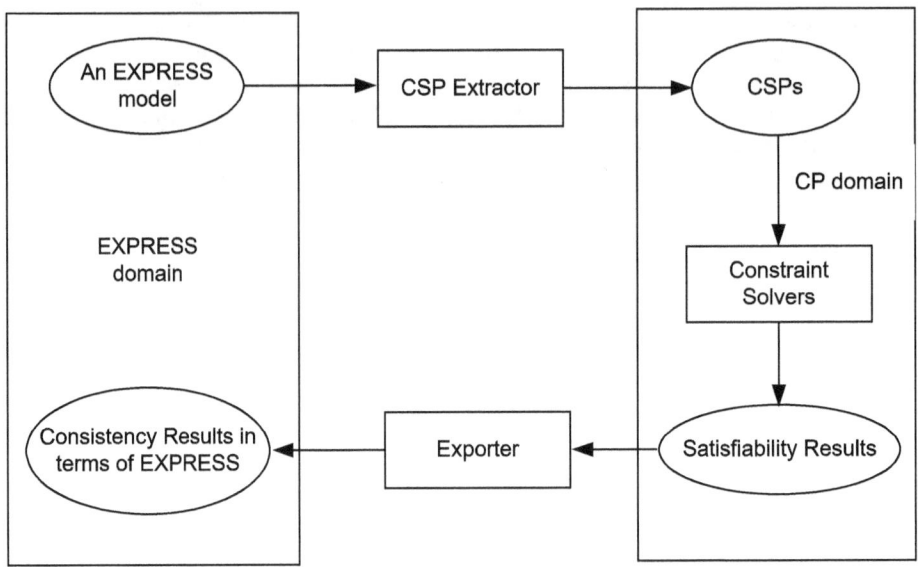

Figure 4.4 Checking EXPRESS Model Consistency with CP

Moreover, most EXPRESS constraint types can be represented in CP. Among twelve constraint patterns in the EXPRESS language, eleven of them can be represented in CP. RULE structures in EXPRESS models cannot be mapped to CP.

No.	*EXPRESS Constraint Types*	*CP*
1	Aggregation datatype (used in attribute declaration) bound specification	Y
2	UNIQUE reserved word in attribute declarations (Uniqueness rules)	Y
3	OPTIONAL reserved word in attribute declarations	Y
4	WHERE rules applied on attributes (Domain rules)	Y
5	RULE structures	N
6	Abstract supertype entity	Y
7	Subtype constraint	Y
8	WHERE rules applied on defined datatypes	Y
9	DERIVE reserved word (attribute derivation)	Y
10	Attribute redeclaration in subtype entities	Y
11	UNIQUE reserved word in aggregation datatype declarations	Y
12	INVERSE reserved word (inverse attribute)	Y

Table 4.4 Comparison between EXPRESS Constraints and CP Constraints

```
Y: CP can represent this EXPRESS constraint pattern;

N: CP cannot represent this EXPRESS constraint pattern;
```

The current research focus, then, is on checking consistency with CP, specifically on correctly, completely and efficiently extracting CSPs from an EXPRESS model. The following sections briefly introduce and explain each of the relevant aspects. Then, more detailed descriptions are provided in the subsequent chapters.

4.3 Checking EXPRESS model consistency by using CP

The approach in Section 4.2.4, exploiting CP in checking EXPRESS models for consistency, has been identified as the most capable one. The research focus is then on how to exploit CP technology in EXPRESS model consistency checking. Figure 4.4 illustrated the initial and primitive idea of checking

EXPRESS model consistency with CP. In that initial version, EXPRESS model consistency checking involves extracting CSPs from the EXPRESS model, passing the extracted CSPs to constraint solvers for satisfiability checking, and finally reporting the consistency results in terms of EXPRESS.

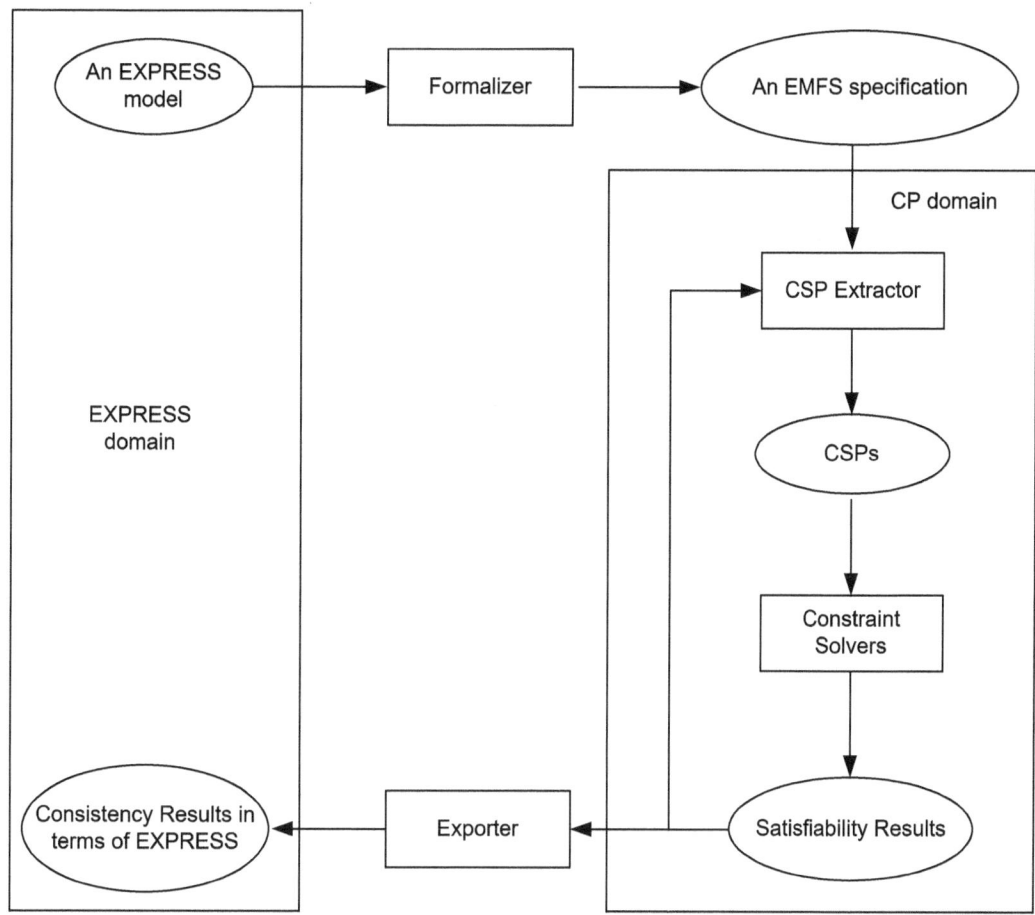

Figure 4.5 The Procedure of Express Model Consistency Checking

Figure 4.5 illustrates the refined checking procedure. Compared with the initial approach illustrated in Figure 4.4, it has two differences. The first difference is that the refined approach includes a formalizer that formalizes the input EXPRESS model to an EXPRESS Model Formal Semantics (EMFS) specification. The second difference is that the satisfiability results are used to control the CSP extractor in the refined approach.

In brief, the procedure for checking consistency of an EXPRESS model using CP has three steps. The first step is model formalization, which extracts the EXPRESS Model Formal Semantics (EMFS) from the model that is to be checked. The second step is then checking the EMFS specification for consistency. The third step is reporting the consistency results in terms of EXPRESS.

CP technology cannot handle RULE structures in EXPRESS models; the research about consistency checking in the following part of this book excludes RULE structures.

4.3.1 EXPRESS model formalization

Formalization, as a step, appeared in Figure 4.5, but not in Figure 4.4, because this step had not been identified initially. As the research work proceeded on and the checking procedure was refined, it was found necessary to formalize the EXPRESS model before checking its consistency.

4.3.1.1 Reasons for Model Formalization

Section 4.1 stated that the EXPRESS language is informal, because it was not developed on the basis of a well-defined formal semantics.

As stated in Chapter 2, consistency issues for a specification are actually the conflicts that exist among its clauses at the semantic level. Identifying inconsistency or proving consistency requires that the piece of specification under scrutiny should be defined by unambiguous and well-defined semantics. CP, as a method for consistency checking, is based on some mathematical and logical theories such as Logic, Artificial Intelligence and Operational Theory. Therefore, to take advantage of the power of CP, it is necessary to formalize the EXPRESS models to bridge between the domains of the EXPRESS language and CP.

4.3.1.2 Formalization tasks

In the context of consistency checking, formalization is to carry out three tasks.

The first task is to separate constraints from data types. Constraints in EXPRESS models are not stand alone, but attached to some data types. However, when composing CSPs for the purpose of consistency checking, only the constraints are used. It is therefore necessary to separate the constraints from the data. For example of the `personModel` schema in Section 3.4:

```
SCHEMA personModel;

ENTITY person;
    howOld: age;
WHERE
    r1: SELF.howOld < 0;
END_ENTITY;


TYPE age = INTEGER;
WHERE
naturalNumber: SELF >= 0;
END_TYPE;

END_SCHEMA;
```

The inconsistency in the above model is between the `r1` and `naturalNumber` WHERE rules. The `r1` WHERE rule is in the `person` entity and the `naturalNumber` WHERE rule is in the `age` defined data type. The CSP that is to be extracted from this model will consist of those constraints `r1` and `naturalNumber`. Therefore before carrying out CSP extraction, `r1` and `naturalNumber` should be separated from `person` and `age`.

The second task is to unify EXPRESS data types to a standard form, and to unify relationships in EXPRESS models to a standard form. Although data types and their relationships are not directly used to compose CSPs for consistency checking, they are important in identifying the intersecting constraint. There are a variety of data types in EXPRESS models, and the relationships among the data types are also various. They are helpful to the expressiveness of the EXPRESS language, but barriers to consistency checking. It is therefore necessary to eliminate the difference among data types and the difference among relationships.

The third task is to transform all EXPRESS constraints to a formal representation, which constraint solvers in CP technology can recognize. In EXPRESS models, special reserved words are used in constraints, which are not acceptable to CP technology. They should be transformed to a CP acceptable form. For example in the `personModel` schema, the `r1` constraint uses the `SELF` reserved word, which is not recognizable to constraint solvers. It must be transformed to a form that constraint solvers understand in order to check consistency.

4.3.1.3 Approach to formalization

For a typical EXPRESS model, formalization is carried out by translating the model to a formal representation. All the components in the EXPRESS model, including data types, entities, attributes and constraints must be translated. In the context of this book, Set theory and FOL are used to capture the EXPRESS Model formal semantics. In brief, the data types in EXPRESS will be mapped to set definitions, the reference and inheritance relationships among data types will be mapped to functions among the corresponding sets, and the constraints will be mapped to predicates in FOL.

4.3.1.4 An example of formalization

The following example shows EXPRESS model formalization.

```
SCHEMA person;
TYPE gender_spec = ENUMERATION OF (male, female);
ED_TYPE;


TYPE age_spec = INTEGER;
WHERE SELF > 0;
END_TYPE;


ENTITY man;
   gender : gender_spec;
   age : age_spec;
WHERE
   R1: age > 20;
   R2: gender = male;
END_ENTITY;


END_SCHEMA;
```

The EMFS specification mapped from the `person` schema consists of three set definitions and two predicates. The sets are:

$$gender\_spec = \{male, female\};$$

$$age\_spec = INTEGER;$$

$$man = gender\_spec \times age\_spec.$$

The first-order-logic predicates are:

$$\forall x \in age\_spec \bullet x > 0;$$

$$R1: \forall <x,y> \in man \bullet y > 20.$$

$$R2: \forall <x,y> \in man \bullet x = male$$

Formal semantics can be drawn from all EXPRESS models in a similar manner to the one shown here, but, as the EXPRESS model grows larger, the formalization becomes more complex. Therefore Chapter 5 will focus on EXPRESS model formalization, explaining all the necessary detail, and describing it formally at a model level.

4.3.2 Checking EMFS specification for consistency

A Constraint Satisfaction Problem (CSP), as introduced in Chapter 2, is a problem of a finite set of variables, each of which is associated with a domain, and a set of constraints that restricts the values the variables can simultaneously take. An algorithm (or a tool that implements the algorithm) for determining the satisfiability of a CSP is called a constraint solver.

EXPRESS model formalization provides a rigid platform for semantics analysis and CSP extraction. From now on, the original EXPRESS model can be put aside; the EMFS specification will be the consistency checking objective. Therefore the second step is checking the EMFS specification for consistency.

EMFS consists of some set definitions and some FOL predicates. A CSP is a set of variables and a set of constraints. Checking an EMFS specification for consistency involves two steps: Extracting CSPs and Solving CSPs. CSP extraction requires the EMFS predicates that refer to the same variables to be identified and then assembled into a CSP of appropriate type.

For the example of the EMFS of the `person` model, the CSP extraction will firstly identify that

$$\forall x \in age\_spec \bullet x > 0$$ and

$$R1: \forall <x,y> \in man \bullet y > 20$$

both refer to a variable in the `age_spec` set, and then, with these two predicates, assemble a CSP:

$$(Z,D,C).$$

$$Z: \{x\};$$
$$D: \{x \rightarrow INTEGER\};$$
$$C: \{x > 0; x > 20\}.$$

Each extracted CSP will go to an appropriate constraint solver for the purpose of satisfiability testing. The consistency in an EMFS specification then involves solving the respective CSPs.

Consider the CSP

$$(Z,D,C).$$

$$Z: \{x\};$$
$$D: \{x \rightarrow INTEGER\};$$
$$C: \{x > 0; x > 20\}.$$

This is sent to an integer constraint solver, and gets a positive result. According to this positive result, a conclusion can be drawn that the EMFS specification of the `person` model in Section 4.3.1 is consistent.

In the context of current research, the external constraint solvers are regarded as black boxes, and are out of the research focus. In order to check EXPRESS model consistency, some constraint solvers are tested and deployed. However, the current research task is not concerned with their contents and does not have a goal of contributing to CP technology. These solvers are regarded essentially as magic boxes, which can solve the input constraints and check the satisfiability of the input constraints. Chapter 7 discusses this topic further.

4.3.3 Exporting results

The EMFS specification consistency should be mapped to the domain of EXPRESS models. The exporter in Figure 4.5 carries out this task.

4.3.4 An example of EXPRESS model consistency checking

Sections 4.3.1, 4.3.2 and 4.3.3 introduce three steps of EXPRESS model consistency checking. This section gives an example to illustrate the checking procedure that integrates the three steps.

Consider the simple electric circuit shown in Figure 4.6. Ohm's law:

$$V = I \times R$$

describes the relationship among voltage V, current I and resistance R in a resistor. Kirchhoff's Voltage Law (KVL) states that the sum of the voltages around any loop in a circuit must equal zero. Dually Kirchhoff's Current Law (KCL) states that the sum of currents entering a junction in a circuit must equal zero. In Figure 4.6, the electric circuit consists of two resistors r1 and r2 which are connected in parallel, and a power source p1.

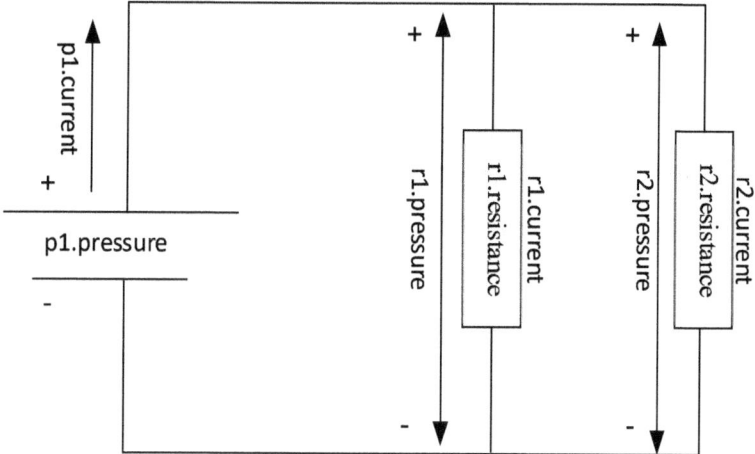

Figure 4.6 Simple Electric Circuit

The following EXPRESS model describes the electrical circuit in Figure 4.6.

```
SCHEMA simple_electric_circuit;

ENTITY resistor;
  pressure: REAL;
  resistance: REAL;
  current: REAL;
WHERE
  ohms_law: pressure=resistance*current;
END_ENTITY;

ENTITY power;
  pressure : REAL;
  current : REAL;
END_ENTITY;

ENTITY circuit;
  p1 : power;
  r1 : resistor;
  r2 : resistor;
WHERE
  p1_r1_parallel_connection: p1.pressure = r1.pressure;
  p1_r2_parallel_connection: p1.pressure = r2.pressure;
  r1_r2_parallel_connection: r1.pressure = r2.pressure;
  kirchhoff_current_law:
    p1.current = r1.current+r2.current;
  r1_r2_equal: r1.resistance = r2.resistance;
  current_r1_great_r2: r1.current > r2.current;
END_ENTITY;

END_SCHEMA;
```

The first step of checking consistency in the simple_electric_circuit schema is to formalize it. The EMFS of that schema consists of some specifications of sets, functions and predicates.

Sets:

R;

$resistor = R \times R \times R$;

$power = R \times R$;

$circuit = power \times resistor \times resistor$.

Functions:

$\text{resistor.pressure} : resistor \mapsto R$;

$\text{resistor.resistance} : resistor \mapsto R$;

$\text{resistor.current} : resistor \mapsto R$;

$\text{power.pressure} : power \mapsto R$;

$\text{power.current} : power \mapsto R$;

$\text{circuit.p1} : circuit \mapsto power$;

$\text{circuit.r1} : circuit \mapsto resistor$;

$\text{circuit.r2} : circuit \mapsto resistor$;

Predicates:

$ohms\_law : pressure = resistance * current$;

$p1\_r1\_parallel\_connection : p1.pressure = r1.pressure$

$p1\_r2\_parallel\_connection : p1.pressure = r2.pressure$

$r1\_r2\_parallel\_connection : r1.pressure = r2.pressure$

$kirchhoff\_current\_law : p1.current + r1.current + r2.current$

$r1\_r2\_equal : r1.resistance = r2.resistance$

$current\_r1\_greater\_r2 : r1.current > r2.current$

The second step involves checking the EMFS specification from the `simple_electric_circuit` schema. The CSPs extracted from the above EMFS are:

CSP 1: (Z_1, D_1, C_1);

Z_1: $\{pressure, resistance, current\}$;

D_1: $\{R\}$;

C_1: $\{pressure = resistance * current\}$.

CSP 2: (Z_2, D_2, C_2)

Z_2: $\{p1.pressure, p1.current,$
$r1.pressure, r1.current, r1.resistance,$
$r2.pressure, r2.current, r2.resistance\}$;

D_2: $\{R\}$;

$$C_2: \begin{cases} p1.pressure = r1.pressure, \\ p1.pressure = r2.pressure, \\ r1.pressure = r2.pressure, \\ p1.current = r1.current + r2.current, \\ r1.resistance = r2.resistance, \\ r1.current > r2.current, \\ r1.pressure = r1.resistance * r1.current, \\ r2.pressure = r2.resistance * r2.current \end{cases}.$$

Those CSPs are then submitted to some external constraint solvers whose applicative domain is real numbers. Then the constraint solver works out the result that `CSP 1` is satisfiable, but `CSP 2` is not. Such a result reflects the truth that in the `simple_electric_circuit` schema the `resistor` entity is consistent, but the `circuit` entity is not.

4.4 The formal and model-based consistency checking description

Section 4.3 briefly and informally described EXPRESS model consistency checking. It used some informal descriptions in natural English and some figures to describe the checking activity. An example was also made to demonstrate the checking procedure. Although that section produced a clear representation that is sufficient for readers to understand the main methods and concepts of EXPRESS model consistency checking, it did not cover all details and did not show the complexity in that approach.

The EXPRESS model consistency checking is formally described and documented in a model-based manner in this section and the following chapters. The model based specifications provide a formal basis for implementation; make the development process traceable and repeatable. They also act as reference models or documentation, and make the developed consistency checking tool consistent and easier to maintain.

The following chapters, which introduce the detail of consistency checking, approach the problem from the perspective of models, including modelling, modelling behaviour and model mapping.

The EXPRESS modelling language family, including the EXPRESS language, the EXPRESS-X language and the EXPRESS-C language [PDTec] are used to define and describe the consistency checking activity.

4.4.1 Model level consistency checking specification

Section 4.3 described the consistency checking activity at the instance level. In other words, it represented the scenario when an EXPRESS model is checked for consistency. At the model level, consistency checking is illustrated in Figure 4.7.

At the model level, EXPRESS model formalization is described as mapping from an EXPRESS meta-model to a model of EXPRESS Model Formal Semantics (EMFS). The model of CSP extractor in EXPRESS-C describes the task that a CSP extractor carries out and the algorithms used to implement that task. The model of EMFS and CSP are referenced by the model of CSP extractor. The model of Exporter in EXPRESS-C, which references the EXPRESS meta-model and the model of CSP, describes how the final consistency results are reported according to the satisfiability results of the generated CSPs. The model of constraint solvers describes constraint solvers at the model level, and is referenced by the model of CSP. In Figure 4.5, there are four components that are used for the purpose of consistency checking: Formalizer, CSP extractor, Constraint Solvers and Exporter. It is possible to develop the Formalizer on the basis of the mapping from the EXPRESS meta-model to the model of EMFS, to develop the CSP extractor, the Exporter and the Constraint Solvers according to corresponding models in Figure 4.7.

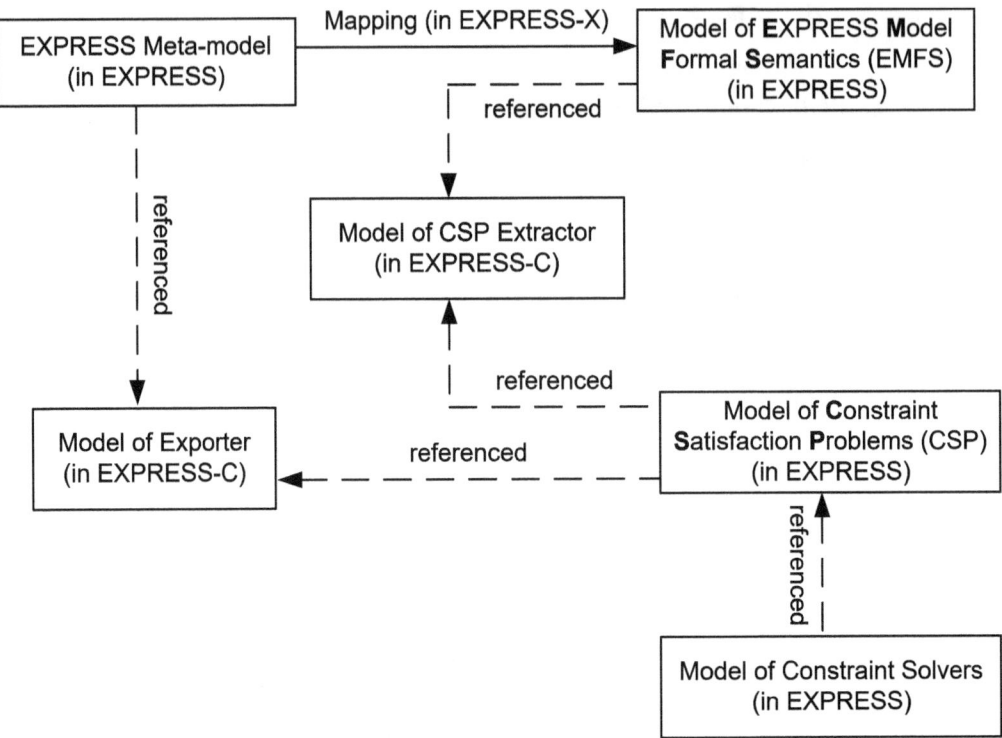

Figure 4.7 Model Level Description of Consistency Checking

The following chapters focus on the models in Figure 4.7. Chapter 5 describes the EXPRESS meta-model, the EMFS model and the mapping from the former to the latter. Chapter 6 focuses on CSP extractor. Although the model of CSP is built in EXPRESS-C, Chapter 6 will use some UML Activity and Sequence diagrams [OMG1999] instead of EXPRESS-C specifications to explain it for the purpose of clear illustration and easy-understanding. The Exporter, will be introduced in Chapter 7.

4.4.2 Mapping specification in EXPRESS-X

The EXPRESS-X language will be used in Chapter 5 to formally describe mappings between EXPRESS models. A brief introduction to EXPRESS-X is necessary before reading the following chapters and for understanding the model mapping approach used.

EXPRESS-X is a general mapping language which is widely used in the STEP domain [Fang]. It is based around some other EXPRESS mapping languages such as EXPRESS-V [Hardwick94], EXPRESS-M [CIMIO]. It is adopted in this research because of its expressiveness and available parsing tools.

EXPRESS-X is a language that maps information between models. A simple description of it is that it is an upward compatible extension of the EXPRESS language that adds some features of SQL. It has two constructs called VIEW and MAP. The former specifies the alternative views of the data described by an EXPRESS information model. The latter, with the assistance of the former, specifies the transformation of data described by elements of one EXPRESS model into data described by elements of another EXPRESS model.

The following two models will be used to illustrate VIEW and MAP structures in EXPRESS-X.

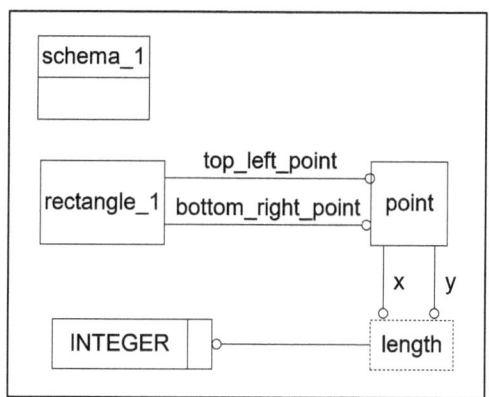 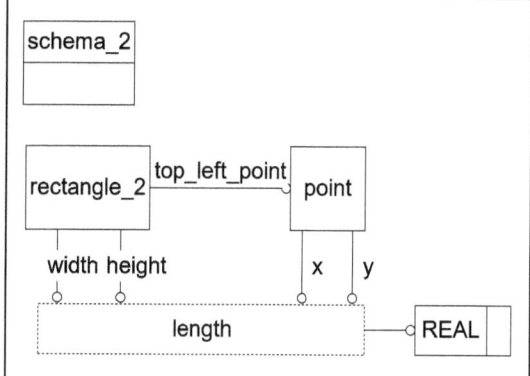

Figure 4.8 Two Models of Rectangle

In Figure 4.8, there are two schemas: schema_1 and schema_2. Below is the description of the models in the EXPRESS language.

```
SCHEMA schema_1;
ENTITY rectangle_1;
        top_left_point     : point;
        bottom_right_point : point;
END_ENTITY;
ENTITY point;
        x : length;
        y : length;
END_ENTITY;
TYPE length = INTEGER;
END_TYPE;
END_SCHEMA;


SCHEMA schema_2;
ENTITY rectangle_2;
        top_left_point : point;
        width : length;
        height : length;
END_ENTITY;
ENTITY point;
        x : length;
        y : length;
END_ENTITY;
TYPE length = REAL;
END_TYPE;
END_SCHEMA;
```

From the names of the entities and attributes in Figure 4.8, both schemas capture the geometrical concept of rectangle. In schema_1, a rectangle_1 entity has two attributes top_left_point and bottom_right_point. In schema_2, a rectangle_2 entity has three attributes topLeftPoint, width and height.

4.4.2.1 View

VIEW is an alternative organization of the information in an EXPRESS model. The example schema_view of the EXPRESS-X language consists of a square_from_rectangle view construct. The square_from_rectangle view reorganizes the information in the schema_2 schema.

(*This is a SCHEMA_VIEW in EXPRESS-X*)

SCHEMA_VIEW example;

REFERENCE FROM schema_2;

VIEW square_from_rectangle;

FROM (p: schema_2.rectangle_2);

WHERE (p.width = p.height)

SELECT

    top_left_point : point := p.top_left_point;

    side_length : length := p.width;

END_VIEW;

END_SCHEMA_VIEW;

In the above example, the SCHEMA_VIEW and END_SCHEMA_VIEW define the scope of a VIEW construct. Information in the FROM language element of the VIEW is used to identify the source extents from which the view is established, and also to define some variables for the latter reference. The FROM element in the above example states that the VIEW is established on the rectangle_2 entity in the schema_2 schema. The variable p is defined too; it is bound to the rectangle_2 entity. One or more selection criteria are applied to each of the instances of the viewed model. The selection criteria are defined by the WHERE language element of the view data type. The WHERE language element from the above example defines a selection criterion identifying a subset of the instances. In this case, the subset of instances for which the value of the width attribute of variable p equals the value of the height attribute of variable p. The SELECT language element defines the attributes of VIEW. In this example, the first attribute, top_left_point, receives its value from the top_left_point attribute of variable p; the side_length attribute receives its value from the width attribute of the variable p. The square_from_rectangle view does not provide any supplementary information beyond the schema_2 schema, but filters the squares from the rectangles.

The view constructs do not carry out the mapping by themselves, but assist the map constructs to do so. The view constructs apply some selection, transformation and construction on the mapping source model, and await the invocation from the map constructs. The mapping may be directly from some entities of the source schemas or from some views of them when the mapping source is not an explicitly defined entity in the source model.

4.4.2.2 Map

The map constructs are the core of the EXPRESS-X language, because they carry out the mapping within the context of the view structures.

The MAP declaration supports the specification of correspondence between semantically equivalent elements of two or more EXPRESS models possessing differing structure. Map is therefore the declaration of a relationship between data of one or more source entity types or view data types and data of one or more target entity types.

A MAP declaration consists of a header and a body. The header identifies target instances to be created and the selection criteria to be applied. The body assigns values to the attributes of these target entities. A MAP construct of the EXPRESS-X language may describe the mapping between the models in Figure 4.8.

```
SCHEMA_MAP rectangle_map;
TARGET tar : schema_2;
SOURCE src : schema_1;
MAP rectangle_to_rectangle AS rectangle_2;
    FROM (p : src.rectangle_1)
SELECT
    rectangle_2.top_left_point := p.top_left_point;
    rectangle_2.width    :=    p.top_left_point.x_p.bottom    -
right_point.x;
    rectangle_2.height   :=    p.top_left_point.y-p.bottom    -
right_point.y;
END_MAP;
END_MAP_SCHEMA;
```

In the above example, the SCHEMA_MAP and the END_SCHEMA_MAP declarations define a scope for a collection of related mapping declarations.

In the MAP construct, the header, MAP rectangle_to_rectangle AS rectangle_2 expressed that the mapping target was rectangle_2 entity.

The body of the mapping:

```
FROM (p : src.rectangle_1)
SELECT
    rectangle_2.top_left_point := p.top_left_point;
    rectangle_2.width    :=    p.top_left_point.x    -
p.bottom_right_point.x;
    rectangle_2.height   :=    p.top_left_point.y    -
p.bottom_right_point.y;
END_MAP;
```

described how to assign the values of the target instances. In detail, the values of three attributes of the rectangle_2 entity: top_left_point, width and length are computed from the mapping source, the rectangle_1 entity in the schema_1 schema. The top_left_point attribute of the rectangle_2 receives the value of the top_left_point attribute of the p variable. The width attribute of the rectangle_2 entity receives the difference between the values of the x attributes of the top_left_point attribute and the bottom_right_point attribute of the p variable. The height attribute the rectangle_2 entity receives the difference between the values of the y attributes of the top_left_point attribute and the bottom_right_point attribute of the p variable.

The Map constructs identify the target entities in their headers, and then in their bodies, assign values to the attributes of the target entities. The assigned values are computed from the values of the attributes of some entities, which are commonly called the mapping source. The Map construct defines the mapping source, the mapping target and the mapping rules, and is the core of the EXPRESS-X mapping language.

4.4.3 Model activity specification in EXPRESS-C

The EXPRESS language only describes the static attributes of a system. One of its extensions, the EXPRESS-C language, can cover dynamic activities. Describing EXPRESS model consistency checking requires not only some static models, but also the modelling of dynamic behaviours. Therefore the EXPRESS-C language is used to describe the EXPRESS model consistency checking.

The principle of the EXPRESS-C language is to extend the EXPRESS language to cover the dynamic properties of application objects using a single specification of information.

The EXPRESS-C language supports the definition and declaration of operations, events and actions.

4.4.3.1 Operation

The EXPRESS-C language supports declaring operations on entities. Each operation has an identifier, optional parameters and an optional return type. This provides a profile of the operation.

An operation on an entity instance is invoked by specifying its identifier with the name of the operation. Then the operation stated will be performed on the entity instance identified. SELF is always passed implicitly as an actual parameter to all entity instance operations.

An operation has a specified algorithm. Because the modeller cannot always specify an algorithm and because of the possible volume of EXPRESS needed, it would not be suitable to include the full algorithm with the profile. The specification of the full algorithm of an operation is optional. The algorithm can be a full specification using the language facilities already available in ISO EXPRESS for the specification of EXPRESS functions and procedures. Operations declared on an entity can be re-declared.

4.4.3.2 Events

An information modeler, working with requirements models and conceptual models, will have no concerns about how an event occurs or how the system handles and generates events. The only property of relevance is the specification of what the event is in declarative form and how the system should react.

There is no specification in this language on how these events occur or how their occurrences are detected. There is only the declaration specification of what the events are and of the conditions under which these occurrences cause the system to react taking specific actions.

4.4.3.3 Actions

An action is an atomic unit. That is all the individual actions that compose it must terminate correctly. Satisfying all the constraints of the system or none of them is considered as completion. An action is a controlled list of operations that can be performed depending on conditions. An action can be invoked directly by an application or it can be invoked as an effect from the occurrence of an event. How this happens is of no concern to EXPRESS-C.

An action when completed must leave the model in a consistent state. If the action is not completed then the model will be returned to its last consistent state before the action started.

An action can have pre and post conditions. There are implicit pre and post conditions in the model that have to be in a consistent state before and after each action. Modelers can add user-defined pre and post conditions.

4.5 Summary

A few approaches to EXPRESS model consistency checking were recognised. The CP-based one, after analysis and comparison, was identified to be the most capable. This chapter then generally introduced a range of considerations related to checking EXPRESS model consistency with Constraint Programming, and the EXPRESS-X and EXPRESS-C languages that are used to formally describe such checking activity.

References

[Abrial]	J. R. Abrial, *The B-Book*, The Cambridge University Press, ISBN 0 521 49619 5 (hardback), 1996.
[ACM]	Association for Computing Machinery (ACM), www.acm.org, September 2004.
[André]	Pascal André, Annya Romanczuk, Aline Vasconcelos and Jean-Claude Royer, *Checking the Consistency of UML Class Diagrams Using Larch Prover*, The Third Workshop on Rigorous Object-Oriented Methods University of York, UK, http://ewic.bcs.org/conferences/2000/objectmethods/papers/paper1.pdf, September 2004.
[Badder2003a]	Franz Badder, Ian Horrocks and Ulrike Sattler, *Description Logics as Ontology Languages for the Semantic Web*, Dieter Hutter and Werner Stephan, editors, *Festschrift in honor of Jong Siekmann*, Lecture Notes in Artificial Intelligence. Springer, 2003.
[Badder2003b]	Franz Badder, Diego Calvanese, Deborah McGuinness, Daniele Nardi, and Peter Patel-Schneider, *The Description Logic Handbook: Theory, Implementation and Applications*, Cambridge University Press, ISBN 0521781760, 2003.
[Barnes]	John Barnes, *High Integrity Software, The SPARK Approach to Safety and Security*, ADDISON-WESLEY, ISBN 0-321-13616-0, 2003.
[Beale]	Stephen Beale, *HUNTER-GATHERER: Applying Constraint Satisfaction, Branch-and-Bound and Solution Synthesis to Computer Semantics*, Ph. D. Dissertation, School of Computer Science, Language Technology Institute, Carnegie Mellon University, 1997.
[Ben-Ari]	Mordechai Ben-Ari, *Mathematical Logic for Computer Science (Second edition)*, Springer, ISBN 1-85233-319-7, 2001.
[Bechhofer]	Sean Bechhofer and Ian Horrocks, *The WonderWeb Ontology language Layer, Report and Tutorial*, IST project 2001-33052 WonderWeb: Ontology Infrastructure for the Semantic Web, 2001.
[BNF]	British National Formulary, *Extended Backus-Naur Notation* (ENBF), http://www.bnf.org, 2004.
[BoldSoft]	BoldSoft, *ModelRun*, http://www.boldsoft.com/products/modelrun/index.html, August 2004.
[Borland]	Borland, *Together*, http://www.borland.com/together/index.html, August 2004.
[Botting]	Richard John Botting, *Java Language Grammar*, http://www.csci.csusb.edu/dick/samples/java.syntax.html, July 2004.
[Bratko]	Ian Bratko, *Prolog programming for artificial intelligence*, Pearson Education, ISBN : 0-201-40375-7 , 2000.
[Chaltsev]	Andrey Chaltsev, http://www.cs.man.ac.uk/~chaltsea/, September 2004.
[Cisco]	Cisco Systems Inc. http://www.cisco.com/univercd/cc/td/doc/cisintwk/ito_doc/ip.htm, September 2004.
[Clark]	Tony Clark, Andy Evans, Stuart Kent, Steve Brodsky and Steve Cook, *A Feasibility Study in Rearchitecting UML as a Family of Language using a Precise OO Meta-Modeling Approach*, The Precise UML Group, http://www.cs.york.ac.uk/puml/mmf/mmf.pdf, September 2004.
[Colmerauer]	A. Colmerauer, An introduction to PROLOG-III, Communication of the ACM, 33(7):69-90, July 1990.

[Cook] Steve Cook, Anneke Kleppe, Richard Mitchell, Bernhard Rumpe, Jos Warmer and Alan Wills, *The Amsterdam manifesto on OCL*, Technical Report TUM-I9925, Technische Universitat Munichen, December 1999.

[Dincbas] M. Dincbas, P. Van Hentenryck, H. Simonis, A. Aggoun, T. Graf, and F. Berthier. *The Constraint Logic Programming CHIP*. In Proceeding of the International Conference on Fifth Generation Computing System, Page 693-702, Tokyo, Japan, December 1988.

[Dresden] Software Engineering Group, Department of Computer Science, Dresden University of technology, *OCL Compiler*, http://www-st.inf.tu-dresden.de/home/html/en/research/index.html, August 2004.

[CFI] CAD Framework Initiative Inc., *Design Representation Programming Interface, Electrical Connectivity, Version 1.0.0*, ISBN 1-882750-01-2, CFI, 1992.

[CIMIO] CIMIO Ltd, *EXPRESS-M Reference Manual*, http://www.cimio.com/Documents/STEP/exm_ug.html, August 2004.

[Evans] A. Evans, R. France, K. Lano and B. Rumpe, *Developing the UML as a Formal Modelling Notation*, Proceedings OOPSLA'97 Workshop on Object-oriented Behavioral Semantics. 1997.

[FaCT] *Fast Classification of Terminologies*, Information Management Group, Department of Computer Science, University of Manchester, http://www.cs.man.ac.uk/~horrocks/FaCT/, July 2004.

[Fowler] Martin Fowler and Kendall Scott, *UML Distilled, A Brief Guide to the Standard Object Modeling language, second edition*, Addison-Wesley, ISBN 0-201-65873-X, 2001.

[Freuder] E. C. Freuder, *Partial constraint satisfaction*, Proceedings 11th International Joint Conference on AI, 1989.

[Fruhwirth] Thom Frühwirth, Slim Abdennadher, *Essentials of Constraint Programming*, Springer, ISBN 3-540-67623-6, 2003.

[Gallier] Jean H. Gallier, *LOGIC FOR COMPUTER SCIENCE: Foundations of Automatic Theorem Proving*, Harper & Row, Publishers, Inc., ISBN 0-06042225-4, 1986.

[Gogolla] M. Gogolla, and M. Richters, *On constraints and queries in UML*. In M. Schader and A. Korthaus, editors, *The Unified Modeling language – Technical Aspects and Applications*, Physuical-Verlag, Heidelberg, 1998.

[Hamie] Ali Hamie, Franco Civello, John Howse, Stuart Kent and Richard Mitchell, *Reflections on the Object Constraint language*. In J. Bezivin and P. A. Muller, editors, *The Unified Modeling Language, UML'98 – Beyond the Notation*. First International Workshop, Mulhouse, France, June 1998.

[Hardwick94] M. Hardwick, D. Spooner, M. Kilty, Z. Jiang, *Mapping EXPRESS AIM's to ARM's Using Database Views: A comparison of Three Approaches*, Technical Report 94041, Rensselaer Polytechnic Institute, Troy, New York, USA, 1994.

[Hoare] C. A. R. Hoare, *An Axiomatic Basis of Computer Programming*, Communications of the ACM, 12:576-580, 1969.

[Hodges] Wilfrid Hodges, *Logic, an introduction to elementary logic, second edition*, Penguin Group, ISBN 0-141-003-146, 2001.

[Hoflehner] Gerolf F. Hoflehner, Daniel M. Lavery and David C. Sehr, *The compiler as a validation and evaluation tools*, Intel Compiler Lab, 2003.

[Horrocks] Ian Horrocks, Ulrike Sattle and Stephen Tobies, *Reasoning with Individuals for the Description Logic SHIQ*, in the Proceeding of the 17th International Conference on Automated Deduction (CADE-17), 2000.

[Horst] John Horst, Elena Messina, Tom Kramer and Hui-Min Huang, *Precise Definition Of Software Component Specifications*. Intelligent System Division, The National Institute Of Standards and Technology, September 2002.

[IBM2004a] International Business Machines, *Jikes*, http://www-124.ibm.com/developerworks/oss/jikes/, August 2004.

[IBM2004b] International Business Machines, *Rational Rose Developer*, http://www-306.ibm.com/software/awdtools/developer/rose/, August 2004.

[ICL] Intel Compiler Lab (ICL), Santa Clara, California, http://www.intel.com/research/mrl/maps/map_sc.htm. September 2004.

[IMG] Information Management Group, Department of Computer Science, University of Manchester, http://img.cs.man.ac.uk/, July 2004.

[ISO91a] International Organization for Standardization (ISO), *Industrial Automation System and Integration, Product Data Representation and Exchange – Part 41: Integrated Resources: Fundamentals of Product Description and Support*, Reference Number ISO TC18/SC4/WG5, ISO 1991.

[ISO91b] International Organization for Standardization (ISO), *Industrial Automation System and Integration, Product Data Representation and Exchange - Part 43: Integrated Resource: Representation Structure*, Reference Number ISO TC184/SC4/WG4 N27, ISO 1991.

[ISO94a] International Organization for Standardization (ISO), *Industrial automation systems and integration –Product data representation and exchange -- part 1: Overview and fundamental principles*, Reference Number ISO 10303-1:1994, ISO, Switzerland, 1994.

[ISO96] International Organization for Standardization (ISO), *Information technology -- Syntactic metalanguage -- Extended BNF*, Reference Number ISO ISO/IEC 14977:1996, Switzerland 1996.

[ISO99] International Organization for Standardization (ISO), *Production Data Representation and Exchange – EXPRESS-X Language Reference Manual*, Reference Number ISO TC184/SC4/WG11 N088, October 1999.

[Jaffar] J. Jaffar, S. Michaylov, P. Stuckey and R. Yap. *The CLP(R) language and system*. ACM Transactions on Programming Languages and Systems, 14(3):339-395, July 1992.

[Jones] Cliff B. Jones, *Systematic Software Development Using VDM*, Prentice-Hall International, ISBN 0-13-880725-6, 1994.

[Klesse] Klesse Objecten, *Octopus*, http://www.klasse.nl/ocl/octopus-intro.html, August 2004.

[Lamport] Leslie Lamport, *A simple approach to specifying concurrent systems*, Artificial Intelligence and Language Processing, Volume 32, January 1989.

[Lano] Kevin Lano and Howard Haughton, *SPECIFICATION IN B: AN INTRODUCTION USING THE B TOOLKIT*, Imperial College Press, ISBN 1-86094-008-0, 1996.

[Leuschel2001] Michael Leuschel, *Design and Implementation of the High-Level Specification Language CSP(LP)*. Proceedings of PADL'01, 3rd International Symposium on Practical Aspects of Declarative Languages, 2001.

[Leuschel2003] Michael Leuschel and Michael Butler, *ProB: A Model Checker for B*, Proceedings of Formal Methods Europe, 2003.

[Levesque] Hector J. Levesque and Ronald J. Brachman, *Expressiveness and tractability in knowledge representation and reasoning*, Computer Intelligence Vol. 3, 1987.

[Lufthansa] The German airline company (Lufthansa), Daysy, day-to-day scheduling Project, http://www.cordis.lu/esprit/src/results/res_area/st/st4.htm, August 2004.

[Marriott] Kim Marriott and Peter J. Stuckey, *Programming with Constraints: An Introduction*, The MIT Press, ISBN 0-262-13341-5, 1998.

[Minsky]   Marvin Minsky, *A Framework for Representing Knowledge*, http://web.media.mit.edu/~minsky/papers/Frames/frames.html, September, 2004.

[Meyer]   Betrand Meyer, Object-Oriented Software Construction, Prentice Hall, second edition, ISBN 0-13-629155-4, 1997.

[Nielson]   Hanne Riis Nielson and Flemming Nielson, *Semantics with application: a formal introduction*, John Wiley & Sons, Inc., ISBN 0-471-92980-8, 1992.

[Nilsson]   Nils, J. Nilsson, *Artificial Intelligence A New Synthesis*, Morgan Kaufmann Publishing, Inc. ISBN 7-111-07885-3, 2000.

[OMG1999]   Object Management Group, *OMG Unified Modeling Language Specification, Version 1.4*, June 1999.

[OMG2004]   Object Management Group, www.omg.org, September 2004.

[PDTec]   PDTec, *ECCO Toolkit*, http://www.pdtec.de/, January 2005.

[Poole]   David Poole, Alan Mackworth and Randy Goebel, *Computational Intelligence: A Logical Approach*, Oxford University Press, Inc., ISBN 0-19-510270-3, 1997.

[Pozrikidis] C. Pozrikidis, *Numerical Computation in Science and Engineering*, Oxford University Press, ISBN 0195112539, 1998.

[Pressman]   Roger S. Pressman, *Software Engineering, A Practitioner's Approach, European Adaptation, Fifth Edition*, McGraw Hill, ISBN 0-07-709677-0, 2000.

[Richters2000] Mark Richters and Martin Gogolla, *Validation UML models and OCL constraints*. UML 2000 – The Unified Modeling Language, Advancing the standard, Third International Conference, York, UK, October 2000, Proceedings, volume 1939 of LNCS, Springer, 2000.

[Richters2001] Mark Richters, *The USE tool: A UML-based specification environment*, 2001. http://www.db.informatik.uni-bremen.de/projects/USE/.

[Richters2002] Mark Richters and Martin Gogolla, *OCL: Syntax, Semantics and Tools*, in *Object Modelling with OCL: The Rationale behind the Object Constraint Language*, Springer, ISBN 3-540-43169-1, 2002.

[Schmuller] Joseph Schmuller, *Teaching Yourself UML in 24 hours*, Sams Publishing, ISBN 0-673-32238-2, 2001.

[Schneider] Steve Schneider, *the b-method, an introduction*, Palgrave, ISBN 0-333-79384-X, 2001.

[SemanticWeb] The Semantic Web Community Portal, http://www.semanticweb.org/, July 2004.

Lesa[Snook] Colin Snook and Michael Butler, *U2B*, School of Electronics and Computer Science, University of Southampton, http://www.ecs.soton.ac.uk/~cfs/U2Bdownloads/U2Bdownloads.htm, August, 2004.

[Sowa2004]   John Sowa, *Semantic Networks*, http://www.jfsowa.com/pubs/semnet.htm, September 2004.

[Sowa1999]   John Sowa, *Knowledge Representation Logical Philosophical and Computation Foundation*, Brooks Cole Publishing Co., ISBN 0-534-94965-7, 1999.

[Spivey]   J. M. Spivey, *The Z Notation: A Reference Manual*, Prentice Hall, ISBN 0-13-983789-X, 1989.

[SRI]   Computer Science Laboratory, SRI International, *Prototype Verification System*, http://pvs.csl.sri.com/, August 2004.

[Sun]   Sun Microsystems, *Java 2 Platform, Standard Edition, Release 1.4*, www.java.sun.com, August 2004.

[Taha]   Hamdy A. Taha, *Operational Research: An Introduction*, Prentice Hall, ISBN 0130323748, 2002.

[Tsang]	Edward Tsang, *Foundation of Constraint Satisfaction*, Academic Press, ISBN 0-12-701610-4, 1993.
[Tsang1990]	Edward Tsang and Nigel Foster, *Solution Synthesis in the Constraint Satisfaction Problem*. Technical Report, CSM-142, Department of Computer Science, University of Essex, 1990.
[Voronkov]	Andrei Voronkov, *Proof-Search in Intuitionistic Logic Based on Constraint Satisfaction and Related Complexity Problems*, Logic Journal of The Interest Group in Pure and Applied Logics (IGPL), http://rpc25.cs.man.ac.uk/voronkov/papers/ljigpl_intuit_constr.ps August "004.
[W3Ca]	W3 Consortium, *Web Ontology Language*, http://www.w3.org/2004/OWL/, July 2004.
[W3Cb]	W3 Consortium, *Extensible Markup Language*, http://www.w3.org/XML/, July 2004.
[W3Cc]	W3 Consortium, *Resource Description Framework*, http://www.w3.org/RDF/, July 2004.
[W3Cd]	W3 Consortium, *RDF Vocabulary Description Language 1.0: RDF Schema*, http://www.w3.org/TR/rdf-schema/, July 2004.
[W3Ce]	W3 Consortium, *Scalable Vector Graphics (SVG) 1.1 Specification*, http://www.w3.org/TR/2003/REC-SVG11-20030114/ Septembert, 2004.
[W3Cf]	W3 Consortium, Hypertext Transfer Protocol (HTTP), http://www.w3.org/Protocols/, September 2004.
[W3Cg]	W3 Consortium, HyperText Markup Language (HTML), http://www.w3.org/MarkUp/, September 2004.
[Wallace]	Mark Wallace, *Constraint Programming*, William Penny Laboratory, Imperial College, 1995.
[Warmer]	Jos B. Warmer and Anneke G. Kleppe, *The Object Constraint Language: Precise Modelling with UML*, Addison-Wesley, ISBN 0-201-37940-6, 1999.
[Watt]	David A. Watt, *Programming language Syntax and Semantics*, Prentice Hall International (UK) Ltd., ISBN 0-13-726274pbk, 1991,
[Williams]	H. P. Williams, *Model Building in Mathematical Programming Second Edition*, John Willey & Sons Inc. ISBN 0 471 90606 9, 1985.
[Wilson]	Leslie B. Wilson and Robert G. Clark, *Comparative Programming languages*, Addison-Wesley, ISBN 0 201 71012 9, 2001.
[Wing]	Jeannette M. Wing, *A Specifier's Introduction to Formal Methods*, Computer, Volume 23, Issue 9, ISSN:0018-9162, September 1990.
[Wirth]	Niklaus Wirth, *What can we do about the unnecessary diversity of notations for syntactical definitions?* Communications of ACM, November 1977, v. 20, no. 11.
[Wittmann]	Martin Wittmann, *Ein Interpreter für OCL*, http://www.pst.informatik.uni-muenchen.de/DA/wittmann/, August 2004.

www.ingramcontent.com/pod-product-compliance
Lightning Source LLC
LaVergne TN
LVHW082244060526
838200LV00046B/2050